2.60

P9-BIN-024

FENCING

About the author

Muriel Bower earned her B.S. degree from the University of California at Los Angeles, her M.A. degree from the University of Southern California, and the title Master of Arms from the National Fencing Coaches Association of America.

She was a nationally ranked fencer when she was competing and has taught and coached both men and women for more than twenty years, during which time her teams often have gained regional or national distinction.

Mrs. Bower is chairman of the National Collegiate Athletic Association Fencing Committee and chairwoman of the United States Collegiate Sports Council Women's Fencing Committee. She served as a special official to the 1964 Olympic fencing events in Tokyo and was manager of the women's fencing team at the World University Games in Russia in 1973. She is a member of the Amateur Fencers League of America, the National Fencing Coaches Association of America, and the United States Academy of Arms.

FENCING

Physical Education Activities Series

Muriel Bower
California State University,
Northridge

Third Edition

Wm C Brown Company Publishers
Dubuque, Iowa

CAMROSE LUTHERAN COLLEGE
LIBRARY

Consulting Editor

Aileene Lockhart
Texas Woman's University

Evaluation Materials Editor

Jane A. Mott
Smith College

Copyright © 1966, 1972, 1976 by Wm. C. Brown Company Publishers

Library of Congress Catalog Card Number: 75-20820

ISBN 0–697–07065–4

NO TOC

All rights reserved. No part of this publication may be reproduced,
stored in a retrieval system, or transmitted, in any form or by any
means, electronic, mechanical, photocopying, recording, or otherwise,
without the prior written permission of the publisher.

Printed in the United States of America

GV
1147
B 68
C. 1

15,532

Contents

The author gratefully dedicates this book
to the memory of her fencing master of many years:

Henri J. Uyttenhove

Foreword

A few short years ago, I was privileged to write the foreword to the second edition of this book. As I noted at the time, the first (1966) edition by Muriel Bower and Torao Mori was a by-product of the experience and observations of the authors at the 1964 Olympic Games in Tokyo, where Mrs. Bower served as an international official and Mr. Mori served as coach of the highly successful Japanese Olympic fencing team. However, the book also reflected both authors' unusual technical knowledge and competitive expertise in fencing, in other sports, and in physical education in general.

Although the second edition carried the names of both the authors, it was prepared solely by Mrs. Bower after the untimely death of Mr. Mori in January 1969. Mrs. Bower's diligence in keeping the book up-to-date is confirmed in the publication of this, the third edition of the book.

To the task at hand Mrs. Bower brings remarkable talents. She initially was trained (as was Mr. Mori) by an extraordinarily able Belgian fencing master, Henri J. Uyttenhove, to whom this book is dedicated. From the beginning, her style featured the modern balance of foot and handwork, agility, and speed that has become characteristic of world-class competitors. At the outbreak of World War II, Mrs. Bower (then Muriel Calkins) was established as a teenage Pacific Coast champion. After the war, having married and raised two sons, she returned to competition to win a well-earned number three ranking in the United States. During this period a small but bright cluster of California women dominated the national fencing scene. Mrs. Bower probably would have gone on, as her contemporaries did, to achieve international recognition in the Olympic and Pan American Games except for an automobile accident that cut short her competitive career in 1951.

Turning her attention to physical education, Mrs. Bower taught fencing for both men and women with much success at the University of Southern California and at San Fernando Valley State College (now California State University at Northridge). Recently her achievements have earned her the type of recognition that even in these liberated days is unusual for women: the National Fencing Coaches Association of America awarded her the coveted diploma of Fencing Master, and the National Collegiate Athletic Association named her chairman of the Fencing Rules and Tournament Committee. (I believe she is the first and perhaps the only woman to chair an official NCAA committee.)

Regarding the book itself, in my opinion *Fencing* is an excellent addition to the growing list of good fencing books available in the United States. It emphasizes fundamentals that will enable the beginner to enjoy foil fencing in a relatively brief span of time and will also provide a sound basis for further growth if the student has higher ambitions in the sport. It is a useful tool for class instruction. Consequently, it can be of enormous help for building the type of fencing development program in the United States—in the schools, the colleges, the centers of adult athletic activity— that has proved so valuable in the countries that have enjoyed the most spectacular international success.

It is of course a truism that neither a fencing book, no matter how good, nor topflight class instruction will produce a world champion. As I have said before, top internationalists in fencing have always been "handmade." But it is obvious that a broad base of national interest and competition greatly enhances the chances of finding potential champions who can be brought to maximum strength by the traditional method of hand-to-hand training by an expert fencing master. Seen in this light, a good book like this one can be of incalculable significance to the development of fencing at all levels in the United States.

Miguel de Capriles
President 1961—1965
International Fencing Federation (FIE)

Preface

This second revision of *Fencing* was written to better achieve the original objective of the book, namely, to provide an inexpensive, concise, comprehensive source of information for students in college or university fencing classes. Its usefulness should, however, extend to any student of fencing. It is intended to be used as a supplement to class or individual instruction.

The size of this book has been increased by adding more illustrations of fencing practice and techniques as well as more detailed information on various aspects of this sport in order to provide a more complete text for the student. Also included are more practice drills to aid in the mastery of various skills; in addition, common errors are discussed. Electric foil fencing is discussed in greater detail than in previous editions because more students are advancing to the competitive level.

The main emphasis in learning to fence should be on learning the sound fundamental skills that are basic to the development of proficiency in fencing. I have attempted to set down the most complete information on foil fencing that can be presented within this space.

This book presents a brief background of the history and development of fencing as well as a general overview of the sport. Reasons for various techniques on both the beginning and more advanced levels are discussed in order to help the student understand the relative importance of each move as it is applied in a fencing situation.

Material in this book is up-to-date in terms of techniques, tactics, and rules. A chapter on the current rules of fencing has been included so that the reader can better understand some of the reasons behind the various skills and tactics practiced; through this knowledge one can perhaps be prepared to compete in classroom tournaments and become a well-informed spectator at a fencing tournament. For the same reasons, basic officiating techniques for both standard and electric foils have been included.

Self-evaluation questions are distributed throughout each chapter. These afford the reader typical examples of the kinds of understanding and levels that he or she should be acquiring as progress is made toward mastery of fencing. The reader should not only answer the printed questions but should also pose additional ones as a self-check on learning.

The death of Mr. Torao Mori, the original coauthor of this book, is deeply regretted. I feel, however, that he would approve of this expanded edition of the text on which we collaborated for the first edition.

What is fencing?

1

Fencing is the historic art of offense and defense with the sword, the object of which is for one fencer to score on another without being scored upon first. Fencing developed into a true sport in the seventeenth century when gunpowder and firearms replaced the sword as the basic weapon. Swordsmanship then developed into a sport in which the objective became the touch and not the kill. Today much of the excitement and romance of the sport of serious dueling remain as the fencer attempts to defend against the opponent's point while at the same time trying to find an opening in the opponent's defense.

Modern fencing has become a safe sport due to the protective clothing and flexible, blunted blade that are always used while participating in any bouts. The objective of fencing is not to inflict an injury but to demonstrate an ability to outmaneuver and touch the opponent.

Fencing is now much faster and requires more refinement of technique than was possible with the heavier, longer, and stiffer weapons used by the earlier fencer.

The rules and manner of fencing reflect its original purpose even though techniques and tactics have undergone many changes through the years. There are three weapons which are used in fencing today: the foil, the épée, and the sabre.

VALUES OF FENCING

Fencing is a vigorous sport that requires and develops stamina, quick reactions, speed and accuracy of movement, and excellent coordination.

Fencing is also a mental game. Once a fencer has practiced the various movements until he or she is physically able to carry out a plan without having to think about how the various parts of the body must move, the real excitement lies in outthinking and outwitting the opponent. The fencer must quickly analyze his adversary's style and then plan his strategy accordingly. Traps must be set for the opponent while being careful to avoid those set by him or her.

In addition to the need for a keen, analytical mind, fencing requires decisive thinking and the courage to assume the offensive at any instant that an opportunity arises. If a fencer delays in building up the courage to move, the exact moment will be lost. By being prepared to move at any time, by forcefully dominating the opponent, and by successfully carrying out plans, the fencer increases self-confidence.

Good sportsmanship is an integral part of fencing tradition. For many years fencing was considered a sport for gentlemen only, and participants were expected to conduct themselves accordingly. Much of this flavor still exists. For instance, etiquette requires that a fencer must acknowledge all touches made against him or her in practice and that any doubtful touches must be refused by the one who attempted to score.

FOIL

The foil, which was designed as a practice weapon, is the weapon with which this book is basically concerned. It is the weapon that is used most commonly by women and is usually the first weapon a man learns to use because it is considered basic to fencing. This does not mean that the foil is only a beginner's weapon to be discarded once a person becomes proficient in its use, for it is probably the most difficult of the three weapons to master and offers a lifelong challenge to men and women alike. Once a fencer learns to use the foil well, one can readily learn to use the sabre and épée, and many fencers enjoy competing in all three weapons.

Although the foil is blunted, it is theoretically a pointed sword capable of inflicting only a puncture wound. A touch is scored if the point of the blade hits any part of the valid target area, which is limited to the torso, from the collar to the groin lines in front, and on the back and sides from the collar to the hips. If the point lands anywhere else, it is "off target" and is invalid. In foil, only those touches that would be potentially fatal in serious dueling are counted. There is no penalty for an invalid hit. Any point hit, valid or not, stops action, and no subsequent hits count until the fencers have stopped and once more resumed fencing. A bout ends when a fencer has been touched five times.

In foil fencing a definite sequence of action should be followed. In such a *phrase d'armes*, a well-executed attack, initiated by one fencer, must be parried or evaded before the defender can safely riposte. This is a logical sequence of action when you consider that if someone were coming toward you with a sharp sword your first consideration would be to defend yourself and then to hit in return. It would be dangerous to attack into an attacker with sharp swords because both fencers could be wounded or killed, so the rules do not favor this type of play.

SABRE

Sabre is related to the old cavalry sabre that men on horseback used as a cutting and thrusting weapon. Today's sabre is a flexible, light blade with a theoretical cutting edge along the length of one side of the blade and one-third of the opposite, or back, side. It also has a blunted thrusting point, so the sabre can be used either as a cutting or thrusting weapon. Touches are scored on the upper part of the body above a horizontal line drawn through the highest points of intersection of the thighs and trunk of the fencer when he is in the on-guard position.

Sabre rules concerning right-of-way are similar to those governing foil in that the well-executed attack must be parried before a riposte is made. The sabre target is larger than that of the foil since the arms and head are also valid targets, so there is a greater variety of actions possible than in foil. Movements are often larger than those of foil due to the enlarged target area and the cutting attacks common in sabre, but precise control is just as vital here as in the other weapons.

ÉPÉE

Épée more closely resembles real dueling than any other weapon. The epee, or dueling sword, is stiffer and heavier than the foil, but it is still a point or thrusting weapon. Points anywhere on the body are valid, and no definite sequence of play must be followed. The first person to hit scores, and if two fencers hit simultaneously, both are declared touched.

ELECTRICAL WEAPONS

The difficulty in accurately judging hits by sight has led to the development of effective electric scoring devices in foil and épée. Electric sabre has not yet been perfected to the point of being practical, but it may be in use in the not too distant future.

Can you name the three types of fencing weapons and describe the basic differences among them?

Fig. 1.1 Weapons: Sabre, Épée, Foil with a Pistol Grip, Electric Foil with a French Grip

The épée machine has been in use for many years. The foil machine was first used for a major international tournament in the 1955 World Championship meet. Both electric foil and épée are now required in most meets.

Electrical épées and foils have a button at the tip that is depressed when a touch is made and records the touch by means of a light and buzzer on a central machine. In electrical épée, only a simple circuit is needed since a point may land anywhere on the body. In foil, however, the problem is complicated by the limited valid target area and by the possibility of off-target hits. The electrical foil scoring machine was developed more slowly than the épée machine because it has to differentiate between fair and foul touches. Over the regular jacket, foil fencers wear a metallic vest that covers only the valid target area. The machine registers with a colored light if the point lands on the valid area and a white light if the point lands anywhere off target.

Equipment and clothing should be checked before crossing blades with an opponent. What safety hazards might be observed and how could you correct the problems?

SAFETY

Fencing is one of the safest sports if simple precautions are observed. It is always a mistake to cross blades with anyone unless each person is wearing the mask and jacket that protect the body, the foil arm, and the neck. Accidents can happen to the unprotected fencer very easily because a fencer can be responsible only for his or her own careful actions. Once a second person is involved, one cannot know exactly how the opponent will move or react, and a fencer is apt to react reflexively to a fast-moving blade in such a way as to endanger his or her opponent's face if it is not protected.

The fencing jacket must be fully buttoned in order to properly protect the neck and torso. Holes should be mended. The mask must have a bib to protect the throat, and the wire mesh must not show spots of rust where a blade could penetrate. Dents should be carefully removed.

The foil tip should be examined frequently to see that it is covered by a strip of adhesive tape one-fourth inch wide and four inches long that must be wrapped around it. If even a small portion of a blade breaks, it must be discarded. Under no circumstances should it ever be retaped and used because a measure of flexibility is lost, and a jagged end remains that could easily cause serious damage. Blades can be replaced by unscrewing the pommel, removing the handle and guard, and putting a new blade in the old mounting.

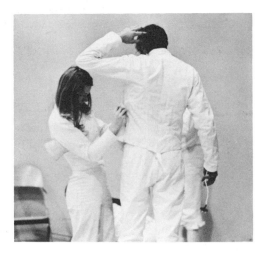

Fig. 1.2   Jackets must be fully fastened for safety. (Photo by Robert Stadd)

Pants that cover the upper leg should be worn rather than shorts. It is very dangerous to fence in shorts, because a blade may end up inside the leg of the shorts and inflict painful groin injuries. There also should be no gap between the lower portion of the jacket and the top of the trousers when the fencer is on guard. In short, all parts that could be hit should be protected.

FENCING SCHOOLS

In the seventeenth century the need for fencing instruction increased as the popularity of dueling grew among the aristocracy. The most important fencing schools originated in Italy, France, and Spain. Each used a different system, and each was considered to be superior by its proponents. The Italian and French systems of fencing proved to be the most widely accepted through the years, and today the influences of these two schools can still be seen. Modifications throughout the years have brought the Italian method, which relied more on power, and the French method, which relied more on finesse, closer together; now the major difference between them is in the shape of the foil handle, which affects the use of the foil.

In this book the French foil is the weapon considered. Although any handle can be used in a similar way, the French handle calls for more finesse and control and is the more balanced foil, making it less tiring to hold. The other grips tend to be more powerful but have a shorter, lighter handle making the weapon point-heavy and thus more fatiguing to hold. Some fencers strap these shorter grips to their wrists for added support, but this limits freedom of movement.

SUGGESTED REFERENCES

BARBASETTI, LUIGI. *The Art of the Foil, With a Short History of Fencing.* New York: E. P. Dutton, 1932.

CASS, ELEANOR BALDWIN. *The Book of Fencing.* New York: Lothrop, Lee and Shephard Co., 1930.

PALFFY-ALPAR, JULIUS. *Sword and Masque.* Philadelphia: F. A. Davis Co., 1967.

Skills basic to fencing

2

Since fencing positions are unlike those of any other sport, it is essential that the beginner take the time necessary to practice the basic moves until they become automatic so that the mind is free to think in terms of acting and reacting to a second, often unpredictable, person.

Although some individual differences are bound to occur, sound basic fencing skills relate to ultimate success in fencing. Various positions and movements have been developed and modified over hundreds of years, so that each position and each action serves a definite purpose. While fencing movements are not difficult, they can become automatic only by continuous repetition. Practicing in front of a capable critic or a mirror is a good way to begin.

At first you will find that the foil feels awkward and unwieldy, but as you become accustomed to its feel, it will become a part of you as you fence. Your movements will tend to be too large at first, also, but with practice they will become small and fast.

THE FOIL

The foil consists of a rectangular blade and its mounting. The blade is not more than 35½ inches in length, with the overall foil being about 42 inches long. The blade tapers from the strong half near the handle, which is called the *forte*, to the weaker, more flexible half, which is called the *foible*. The forte is used for the defense since it is thicker and more rigid than the tip end of the blade. The tip of the standard foil is blunted and must

Are you able to grip the foil correctly by feel alone without looking at the handle?

be covered with a rubber tip or with white tape. Foil blades come in sizes from one to five, size one being the shortest.

Adult preference has usually been for a number five blade, but more fencers are now using a number four. Since electric blades are somewhat heavier and more point-heavy than nonelectric blades, the number four blade, which is one inch shorter, provides better balance and control. It is logical to begin fencing with the same length blade you are likely to use as an advanced fencer.

The mounting consists of the guard, or bell, a thumb pad, the handle, and the pommel, which acts as a counterbalance.

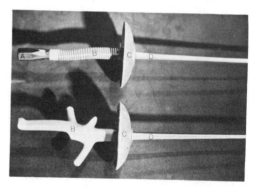

Fig. 2.1 Foils—Top is a French foil and below is a pistol grip foil. A. Pommel; B. Handle; C. Bell Guard; D. Blade. (Photo by Robert Stadd)

How to Hold the Foil

The rectangular French handle is not straight. The right-handed foil should be held so that, with the wider sides on the top and bottom, the handle will curve upward and to the right near the guard.

With the handle in this position, place the last joint of the thumb on top, about one-half inch from the guard. Place the second joint of the forefinger on the bottom so that it opposes the thumb. It is with these fingers that you will guide the foil. Now rotate the hand so that the knuckle of the thumb is at two o'clock. The remaining three fingertips should rest on the left side of the handle where they will add strength to the grip.

The foil must be gripped lightly yet firmly because a heavy or tense grip will result in large motions and will cause undue fatigue. The ability to manipulate the point with the smallest, quickest possible motions will depend on this relaxed but firm grip while the fingers guide the point. When you beat your opponent's blade or defend yourself, you will find

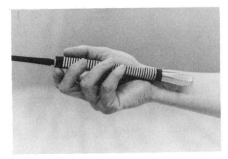

Fgi. 2.2   How to Hold the French Foil.   Fig. 2.3   How to Hold the Pistol Grip
Foil. (Photo by Robert Stadd)

that your fingers must tense to provide additional force, but they must relax when your blade is once more free.

The pommel lies against the center of the wrist so that the foil becomes an extension of the arm with no up or down break at the wrist. (All directions in this book will be for the right-handed fencer. Left-handed fencers should reverse these instructions.)

THE ON-GUARD POSITION

The Salute

Whenever fencers are about to cross blades, whether in a lesson, a practice session, or a tournament, etiquette demands that they salute, so the salute

Fig. 2.4   Preparation to Salute.
The mask is held in the unarmed
hand, heels together at right
angles, guard to the chin.

Fig. 2.5   Salute. The point is brought down
to eye level as the arm is extended toward
the opponent. (Photo by Robert Stadd)

may be considered the standard preliminary to the on-guard position, which is the basic stance preparatory to the attack or for defense. To begin the salute, fencers face each other, foil in hand, with the mask held under the left arm by the back piece, or tongue. The feet should be at right angles, with the right heel directly in front of the left heel and the right foot pointing in the direction of the other fencer. The left foot points to the side.

The salute is made in three quick, smooth motions. On count one, the foil arm is extended toward the floor; on count two, the foil comes up so that the guard almost touches the chin, point up; and on count three, the sword arm is extended shoulder high, with the point aiming at your opponent. After this quick salute, the mask is put on with the left hand, which is already holding it. The proper way to put the mask on is to put the chin in first so it rests on the chin pad, then to pull the mask up and back over the top of the head in one quick motion. This method of putting on the mask not only looks nice but also wastes very little time and tends to pull the hair back away from the face, which is important to those who have hair long enough to hang in their eyes.

The Leg Position

Now you are ready to assume the guard position in one motion. This stance will be broken down into its various parts so it can be learned bit by bit, but once you have become familiar with this position, it should be assumed quickly after the salute.

Fig. 2.6 The On-Guard Position. (Photo by John Kedroff)

Can you identify the French foil?
Can you name the parts: A, B, C, D?

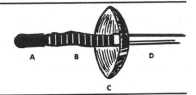

The feet always remain at right angles with the right heel directly in front of the back one, but in the guard position, the forward foot is moved ahead so that there is about a shoulder-width distance between the feet. Both knees bend so that they are over the toes with the body in the center, weight evenly distributed over the balls of the feet. In assuming this bent-knee position, be careful that only the legs move as the body is lowered. The body must not lean forward or backward; the pelvis should be directly under the trunk with shoulders and hips level.

The Arm Position

To bring the arms into position, carry the left arm behind the head. It should be bent at right angles, with the elbow shoulder high and the hand relaxed and hanging forward at about head level. In this position the left arm provides balance, helps keep the body in proper alignment, and is out of the way so it will not be hit. If kept in proper position, it will also add impetus to the attack and act somewhat like a rudder, as will be seen later on in the discussion of the lunge.

Fig. 2.7   The On-Guard Position —Front View. (Photo by Robert Stadd)

The right, or sword, arm is bent so that the elbow is about 8 inches in front of the body, with the hand held at chest level and the point at the height of the opponent's chin. You are now in the guard position.

In the guard position your body should be quite stable with no tendency to fall forward or backward, for you have lowered your center of gravity by bending your knees; the wide stance gives you a firm base of support with your body balanced in the center, hips under the trunk.

The sideways stance puts the sword in front where you will be in position to get maximum reach in the attack and where the arm will help to protect you since the right elbow should be in front of your body. This position also narrows the target, but it is a mistake to take an extreme sideways position in order to further minimize the target. If you find you have difficulty keeping the front foot and knee straight, you may turn the torso from the pelvis up to face slightly forward so that the knee and foot are in a natural position. An extreme sideways stance will restrict your attacking distance and will tend to cause your forward foot and knee to turn in. While such a stance offers a minimum target, it also partially exposes your back, a valid target that is not as easily defended as the front of the target, making this not only an uncomfortable but an impractical position. If you come on guard, facing yourself in a mirror, your left arm should be just visible behind and beside your head.

FOOTWORK

The sport of fencing is only remotely related to the swashbuckling style of swordplay seen in the motion pictures, in which actors turn in circles, leap over tables, and swing from chandeliers. The surface on which you fence is called a *strip*. The foil strip is 2 meters (6 feet, 7 inches) wide and 14 meters (46 feet) long, and fencers are free to move back and forth as long as they remain on the strip and do not reverse positions. Fencers are quite mobile on the strip, and excellent endurance is required to fence for any length of time due to the speed of the fencers' footwork as they move up and down the strip, each trying to draw the other a little too close, keeping on the move so that the other cannot have a chance to get set to attack at leisure, and each trying to get the other a little off-balance so a swift attack can be successfully launched.

Advance

The advance brings you closer to your opponent. It is made by moving the forward foot ahead first about one shoe length with a heel-toe, walking step, then advancing the back foot the same distance. It is best to take short steps as you advance so you do not accidentally step into an attack or get too close to your opponent.

The advance is made in order to get close enough to attack if the opponent is out of distance. It also may be used to maintain a constant distance if the opponent has retreated or to force the opponent to retreat.

The advance should be a fast, smooth, gliding motion. There should be no up-or-down bobbing of the head, no jerky leaping motions, and no dragging of the feet that will slow the footwork. The weight is carried on the balls of the feet, and the back foot provides speed by pushing you forward as you advance.

Retreat

The retreat is the reverse of the advance. It is done by first moving the left foot and then the right foot back about one shoe length. The feet should be the same distance apart at the end of the advance or retreat as they were originally.

The retreat may be used to make the opponent advance or to take you out of attacking distance as you defend against an attack. The retreat also should be made with a gliding motion.

Lunge

The lunge is the extension of the guard position; its purpose is to reach the opponent. It is the basic attacking position that brings you close enough to touch and in position for a quick recovery to the guard position at your regular fencing distance.

How to Lunge   All movements of the arm or blade must start with the point, which is guided into the desired position by the thumb and forefinger. The lunge also must start with the point, which is aimed at the exact spot you hope to hit by pushing down on the handle with the thumb. Once the point is in line, the arm should be quickly and smoothly extended from the shoulder, with the hand slightly higher than the point. The shoulder must not be tensed or lifted because this will shorten your reach by at least an inch and cause your point to jump, spoiling your aim. Reach, rather than push, the blade forward.

This smooth, fast extension should be practiced until it becomes natural and easy before the lunge itself is practiced.

Once the arm is working well, go on to the footwork of the lunge. Aim, extend the arm, then reach forward with the right foot and at the same time drive your body forward with the back foot, which remains flat on

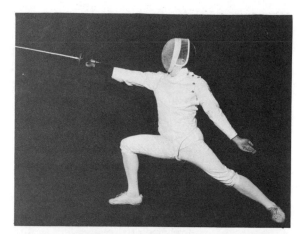

Fig. 2.8   The Lunge. (Photo by John Kedroff)

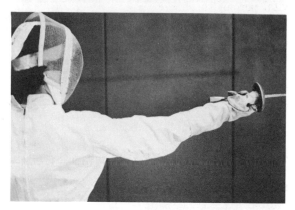

Fig. 2.9   In the lunge, the shoulder and arm are relaxed, arm extended, hand shoulder high. (Photo by Robert Stadd)

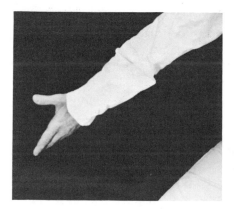

Fig. 2.10   Lunge. The left arm extends directly over the extended leg, palm up. (Photo by Robert Stadd)

Fig. 2.11   Lunge. The forward knee is over the heel. (Photo by Robert Stadd)

Do you know why it is important to take short steps as you advance? If you lift or tense your shoulder, what will be the effects on your attack?

---

the floor during the lunge in order to maintain stability. The main force of the lunge is provided by the powerful extension of the left leg, which drives you forward. The left leg works much like a strong spring that is compressed as you crouch in the guard position, and hurls you forward as the spring, your leg, is released. The driving force that propels you forward must push straight forward through the hips, never up and forward.

At the same time the left leg extends, the left arm is flung down and back, palm up, so that it is in line with, and parallel to, the left leg. This backward extension of the arm helps provide force to the lunge and is a vital part of the lunge, for it quickly displaces your body weight forward. If the left arm moves sideways when you lunge, you will find that you easily can lose your balance in the direction the arm moves. The arm extends straight down.

At the end of the lunge, your body should be in the following position: right knee bent directly over the right instep, not over or in front of the toe because this will put undue strain on the knee and thigh and slow your recovery; hips still under the trunk, facing almost forward; trunk straight but leaning a little toward the point; shoulders level; both arms and left leg straight; and left foot flat on the floor.

Recovery from the lunge is made by pushing from the right heel while pulling the body back with the recoiling rear leg. At the same time, return both arms to a bent guard position. Be sure to bend the left leg when you recover so that you will be in your beginning stance, never standing upright. It takes much less energy to return to a crouch position than to a standing one, and only in this lower position are you ready to continue fencing, which may be necessary if your attack did not land.

How to Practice the Lunge   At first the lunge should be made slowly and analyzed at each step until you are sure you understand how to lunge correctly. You will need to stretch gradually until you can perform a full, deep lunge without feeling any strain. As soon as you can do this slowly, you should begin working for speed and force, which can be acquired only through continuous repetition. Many top-ranking fencers lunge at least one hundred times daily to keep themselves flexible, fast, and in good condition.

Fencers today rarely remain static on the strip. You will need to be able to cover ground quickly, either forward or backward; therefore the advance, retreat, and lunge should be practiced until they become natural movements for you. Then try various combinations of these actions.

Ask your partner to advance repeatedly so as to shorten the distance between you. Can you retreat quickly and just far enough to regain your
proper fencing distance despite variations in the distance your partner
moves forward?

Advance-Lunge

In an advance attack, the sword arm must be extended at the start of the
advance, since this is the beginning of the attack, and it must remain extended throughout the attack. Any time the arm is withdrawn during an
attack, the attacker may be hit by a quick thrust from the other fencer, so
to make this attack, you should first extend as you start to advance, then
lunge with no hesitation between movements.

It often is necessary to attack in this way since much fencing today is
done out of distance, so a lunge will not reach the opponent. This is a
safer distance for fencing since it gives more time for the defense, but it
does require the ability to cover this distance with great speed.

The advance attack is also useful against the opponent who, though
perhaps within fencing distance, habitually retreats as you attack, thereby
making it necessary to gain extra distance in the initial advance. It is essential that you keep all parts of your body under control throughout any
actions you make. If you overlunge or lose your balance in any way, it may
be relatively easy for your opponent to score; so while all-out speed and
determination are required in the attack, your body must always be controlled by keeping your left foot firmly on the floor during the lunge and
by balancing correctly.

Lunge, Recover Forward, Lunge

If your opponent has retreated just out of reach as you lunge, you may recover forward from the lunge by bending the left leg and bringing it forward to put you in the guard position. From this position you can defend,
advance to a better position, or immediately lunge again to score.

You may now try any combination of these actions: advance-lunge-
recover forward-lunge; advance-lunge-recover backward-retreat; and so forth.

FENCING DISTANCE

Fencing distance, or the distance between two fencers, depends on the
length of the lunge. Fencers should be far enough apart so that a full lunge
can just reach the opponent. You should never be on guard closer than

Fig. 2.12 (above) Correct Fencing Distance. (Photo by Robert Stadd)

Fig. 2.13 To find lunging distance, place your point against a wall or fencer from a guard position. (Photo by Robert Stadd)

Fig. 2.14 Then move back, extending the arm, point still touching the surface, then lunge backwards. Recover backwards to lunging distance. (Photo by Robert Stadd)

this distance or you will be too easily scored upon, but you may fence farther apart if you desire. It is important that you quickly become accustomed to your lunging distance so that you will not make the mistake of fencing too closely, a mistake common to beginners. If your opponent has a longer lunge than you have, you should fence at the distance of the longer reach.

To learn your lunging distance you may practice by placing the tip of your foil against a wall, lunging pad, or partner and extending your arm as you assume a guard position so that, with your arm extended, the foil reaches the target with a slight bend in the blade. From this position, reach backward with the back leg until you are lowered into a full lunge. Now, without moving the back foot, recover backward to your guard position which will put you at your lunging distance from the target. Lunge several times, being careful not to allow the back foot to creep forward. Be aware of the distance as you learn just how far you can reach with a full lunge.

Practice Drills

Find your lunging distance from a partner, preferably one of the same general height as yourself. Study this distance until you feel familiar with it. Next, one of you should take the initiative in advancing or retreating, *one step at a time*, while the other fencer maintains a constant fencing distance by retreating as the partner advances or vice versa. The object of this exercise is to learn to adjust your distance quickly and evenly with proper footwork. Be careful to maintain your body weight evenly between your feet, rather than shift it from foot to foot as you move.

Common Errors
1. Moving the wrong foot first in an advance or a retreat. Always move the front foot first to advance and the back foot first to retreat.
2. Moving one foot farther than the other during the advance or retreat. Each must move the same distance.
3. Shifting your body weight over one foot or the other as you move. Keep your weight balanced between your feet at all times.
4. Taking large steps as you move. Several small steps are better than a few long ones.
5. Locking the elbow, thereby slowing a subsequent action.

ENGAGEMENT

Contact of the foibles of the blades for protection while in the guard position is called *engagement* of the blades. When fencers are lunging distance apart, they may engage blades. If your opponent's blade is to the left of yours, you would move your blade left so that a simple lunge could not land against you, and if the blade is to the right of yours, you would move your blade right to protect that line. If two right-handers or two left-handers are working together, they will both be engaged in the same line.

How could this engagement be changed from six to four? Should the point or the hand move first to the new position?

In the engagement, contact should be made lightly with no pushing of the blades. With this light contact, your fingers are sensitive enough to feel the slightest movement made by your opponent's hand even before you can see the motion.

Lines of Engagement

The target is theoretically divided into four lines, or sections: high inside, high outside, low inside, and low outside. The upper lines are above the foil hand, and the lower lines are below it. The inside lines are toward the front of the body, or to the left of the sword hand for right-handers, and the outside lines are toward the back, or to the right of the sword hand. The hand moves left or right as necessary to protect the target.

There are two guard positions for each line: one with the hand in supination, in which the palm faces up, and one in pronation, or palm down. The supination parries are the ones usually used in foil fencing, while the pronation parries are used often in sabre. With the four supination positions you can readily protect any area of the target.

Four   The high-inside line is that of four, or *quarte*. The hand moves to the left until it is in front of the left side of the body, point over the edge of the opponent's right shoulder. In this position, the wrist breaks laterally so the pommel is not against the wrist, but the handle remains under the base of the thumb. The thumb knuckle is at one o'clock.

Six   The high-outside line is six, or *sixte*. The hand moves to the right so that it is in front of the right side of the body, point over the opponent's left shoulder. This tends to be a weaker position than four for many people, much as the backhand stroke in tennis is often weaker than the forehand. In order to assure a strong six position, rotate the hand slightly to the right so that the knuckle of the thumb is at two o'clock,

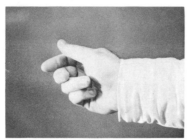

Fig. 2.15 Hand Position of Fourth. (Photo by Robert Stadd)

Fig. 2.16 Hand Position of Fourth. (Photo by Robert Stadd)

Fig. 2.17 Parry Four. (Photo by Ric Thompson)

Fig. 2.18 Sixth Hand Position. (Photo by Robert Stadd)

Fig. 2.19 Sixth Hand Position. (Photo by Robert Stadd)

Fig. 2.20 Parry Six. (Photo by Ric Thompson)

Fig. 2.21   Seventh Hand Position.
(Photo by Robert Stadd)

Fig. 2.22   Parry Seven. (Photo by Ric
Thompson)

Fig. 2.23   Eighth Hand Position.
(Photo by Robert Stadd)

Fig. 2.24   Eighth Hand Position.
(Photo by Robert Stadd)

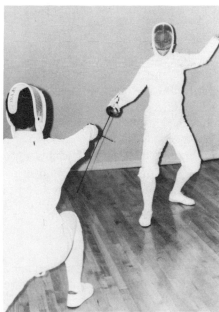

Fig. 2.25   Parry Eight. (Photo by Ric
Thompson)

Fig. 2.26   The Thrust. The arm is extended with the hand shoulder high and the point slightly lower than the hand.

and brace the pommel against the inside of the wrist for additional support. In this position there should be a straight line from the elbow through the foil.

Seven   Seven, or *septime,* defends the low-inside line. From the high lines of four or six, the move to seven is made by breaking the wrist downward as the point moves clockwise, stopping just beyond the opponent's knee. The hand is to the left of the body as it was in four, still at chest height with the palm of the hand facing up.

Eight   The guard of eight, or *octave,* defends the low-outside line. From four or six, the blade moves counterclockwise, stopping at the inside of the opponent's knee. The hand pivots to the new position as the wrist breaks down, palm of the hand up. The forearm does not drop.

Fingering

Fingering refers to the manipulation of the foil tip by the action of the thumb and forefinger only. It is essential for a fencer to be able to move the point in this manner so that there will be no superfluous motion that is time-consuming and enables the opponent to see what you are doing more easily.

Change of engagement is made by passing the point of the foil under the opponent's blade to engage it on the opposite side. The point must move the smallest distance with very delicate fingering. The point should move first to contact the other side of the blade, and then the hand moves to the new guard position.

The change is useful in maintaining control over your opponent's foil. If, for instance, you feel that the other fencer is about to attack, a quick change of engagement may upset his plans. You may change engagement in order to get control of the other blade prior to attacking or when advancing to maintain blade contact and lessen chances of an attack that may be initiated against you when you advance.

Double change of engagement consists of two rapid changes of line without moving the hand. A proficient fencer often attacks as his opponent advances, because for a brief instant he cannot retreat out of distance. A quick double change as you advance makes it very difficult for the other person to attack. The double change can be used in the same way that a single change is made. These actions should both be used, but not continuously. Remember that you must always keep the opponent guessing as to what you will do next, so you must be careful to avoid doing any one thing repeatedly.

The double change is good fingering practice because it strengthens the fingers. It also requires a relaxed grip; therefore it can serve as a reminder to keep your hand and arm loose as you fence.

Practice Drills

Working with a partner, change engagement several times while he holds a steady guard position in four or six. Next, practice the double change of engagement in the same manner, and then reverse roles. Repeat this drill, but advance just after the point moves to change or double change. Your opponent should retreat as you advance to maintain correct fencing distance. Work for speed, finesse, and ability to control an opponent's blade without trying to push or move it.

DEFENSE

Parries

The defense with the blade is called a *parry*. This may be either a blocking parry, which is made by moving the sword to protect yourself by blocking the attack, or a beat parry, which is made by spanking the opponent's blade sharply. The blocking parry is more useful against a powerful attack, against a fencer who is too close, or against one who tries to hit by jabbing repeatedly. The beat parry is more useful against a clean attack because it frees your blade so that you may immediately score after your defense.

Either type of parry is made by moving the point and hand to the desired line, so that you may parry in four, six, seven, or eight. There must be no backswing and no follow-through, either of which would momentarily expose your target and consume additional time. The flexible tip of the blade whips laterally at any sharp impact, but it will quickly right itself if the hand is kept under careful control. Any large motions will result in still more point deviation, making it very difficult to guide the point accurately. You must try to stop the point just over the edge of your opponent's shoulder in the high lines, or beside the knee in the low lines. From the proper parry positions, you only need to aim the point and quickly extend to score after a successful defense.

When a parry is made, the sword arm should neither extend nor bend from the guard position unless the opponent is closer than the normal fencing distance, in which case the arm will have to be withdrawn in order to parry. All parries should deflect the opponent's blade to the side, never up or down, for this may result in an invalid touch to the legs or head. The target is longer than it is wide, so the quickest, shortest parry is lateral.

When parrying, always meet your opponent's blade with a corner of your blade rather than with its flat side; the smaller surface of an edge can deliver more force for a beat or parry. Proper hand position will assure such a blade position.

Types of Parries

Direct parries are made by moving the sword to the left or right to defend either the high or low lines. If a fencer is on guard in six, the line of four will be open, so an attack to the line of four may be defended by the direct parry of four.

Semicircular parries are made when moving from high to low or from low to high lines, since the tip of the blade describes an arc as it crosses the body to remove the threatening blade laterally.

Circular or Counter parries are made by changing lines with a small, circular motion of the blade, so that an attack to the high-inside line of four can be parried by the direct parry of four, or by counter six.

The circular parries may seem to be slow, but they can be made very quickly. For instance, if a fencer is on guard in four, the high-outside line of six will be unprotected, so an attack to this open line can be parried with counter four. Since the hand is already in the position of four, the arm need not move. The thumb, forefinger, and wrist will guide the point under the blade to pick it up in four with a quick, small, powerful parry.

It is important for a fencer to be able to make either a direct or circular parry in any line and to vary his use of them. You will find that any time an opponent can accurately predict what you will do, that is, how you will attack or parry, he can score, so outwitting your opponent is a major part of fencing. Changing your defense is one way of keeping the other person guessing, thereby making it more difficult for him to plan his attack.

Practice Drills

Take a guard position in six with your body parallel to a wall, rear toe and knee touching the wall. Quickly move to parry in four. Do not crash into the wall, but stop with the guard and point just touching the wall. Repeat, moving from seven to eight. Next, turn your back to the wall, front foot and back heel about three inches from the wall, and similarly parry from four to six, and from seven to eight.

Engage blades with a partner, making sure that you are the correct fencing distance apart. Begin with the guard of four so that you both guard the upper-inside line of four with your partner's blade to the left of yours. (If one partner is left-handed, his hand will be in six.) Beat the other blade without moving your arm, then allow the partner to beat your blade. Take turns beating in four, being careful to maintain point control.

One partner may change engagement to six and repeat the drill in that line, then similarly beat in the lines of seven and eight. As a progression, one partner may lunge to the fourth line as the other fencer defends in four. Take turns attacking this way in each of the four lines.

Common Faults

1. Taking a backswing, which results in too large an action.
2. Parrying further than necessary, thereby exposing the target rather than covering it.
3. Parrying with a windshield-wiper action so that the parry beats the attacking blade down rather than sideways. Think of the blade as a wall that moves laterally to protect a line.

ATTACKS

Touching the Opponent　　Before actually attacking another person, it is important to learn to make a soft touch as opposed to a hard or jabbing touch.

The action that touches the opponent is called a *thrust*. It is advisable to first thrust at a wall target by taking the guard position just far enough away so that, by extending your arm, you will reach the target firmly

---

In thrusting at a wall target from the guard position, can you make a soft touch on your point of aim 5 successive times without error? 7 times? 10 times? Can you do the same from full lunging position?

---

enough to cause the blade to bend slightly upward. Once the feeling of thrusting with the arm is acquired, the same thing should be tried from the full lunging distance. The thrust should be firm and quick, but not hard.

When you are thrusting well with a full lunge, do the same thing against another person. As soon as possible, you must develop the feel of placing the point on the target with the fingers, and you must learn to be touched without flinching. A good way to practice at first is for partners to get on guard, lunging distance apart, and to take turns lunging and touching each other without attempting to defend themselves. Later the defense may be added as attacks increase in speed and skill.

Simple Attacks

Simple attacks are those consisting of only one fast action. These attacks rely on speed, proper distance, and surprise or timing. There are three simple attacks.

Straight Thrust   This is a fast lunge with no change of line during the attack. It is occasionally a very good attack but cannot be used often against a good fencer.

The straight thrust can be used against an opponent who is not protected in the guard position. Fencers often fence with "absence of the blade," which means that they do not engage blades while on guard but leave the line to which the opponent's blade points unprotected. This is most common when fencing out of distance or more than lunging distance apart. If you can maneuver such a fencer to within fencing distance, it is often possible to score with an explosive straight thrust.

Disengage   When the line in which you are engaged is closed, or protected, you may change lines to hit with a disengage. This movement is made by guiding the point under the opponent's blade with the fingers making the smallest motion needed to clear the blade, then reaching and lunging. It should be made as one continuous motion. The blade stays close to the opponent's blade so that the action will be fast and difficult to see.

The tip of the blade should describe a **V** in this attack. First, the fingers drop the point to the lower point of the **V** without moving the arm

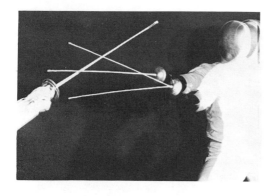

Fig. 2.27 Disengage. 1. Starting position blades engaged in four; 2. Point passes under the blade as the arm extends; 3. Point aims and fencer lunges to hit in the sixth line. (Photo by John Kedroff)

and then aim to the top of the **V** while extending the arm, and finally the fencer lunges. This is one continuous, smooth motion. You may disengage from any line to any other unprotected line, low or high, but when changing from seven to eight, or from eight to seven, the disengage will be made over the blade rather than under it.

Hitting with Opposition   If fencers are engaged in four, their hands are to the left of their torsos. When one of them makes a disengage to six, the hand should change to the position of six when the arm extends, so that the attacker's blade opposes the defender's blade, thereby protecting the attacker's target during the attack.

You must be sure to make the line change before lunging so that there will be no tendency to withdraw the arm during the attack.

Common Faults
1. Lunging before aiming or extending the arm. Always lead with the point, not the foot.
2. Moving the arm and/or point in a wide **U** rather than a small **V**.
3. Withdrawing the arm during the change of line.

Cutover, or Coupé

The cutover consists of lifting the point until it just passes over the other blade, extending, and lunging, all in a continuous motion, with the blade in opposition. This may be effective against a slightly low but not threatening point or when the opponent applies pressure to your blade.

Common Faults
1. Lunging before the point is aimed, causing the arm to withdraw too far.
2. Bending the elbow as the point lifts to clear the tip of the opponent's blade.

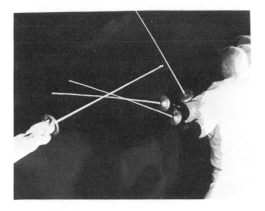

Fig. 2.28 Cutover (Coupé). 1. Starting position with blade engaged in four; 2. Point lifts over the other blade; 3. Point aims and arm extends to score in sixth line. (Photo by John Kedroff)

Compound Attacks

Any attack made up of two or more actions is a compound attack. In such an attack, one or more preparatory actions are followed by the final or thrusting part of the attack. In any such attack, the attacker gains right-of-way by extending his arm but may lose it if he bends his arm during the attack, so in these attacks the arm must be extended or extending. The arm need not be fully extended to gain right-of-way, but it must be *extending*, preferably before lunging. An advance is not an attack, nor is a lunge in which the arm does not at least partially extend an attack.

Preparatory Actions   **Feint.** This motion is intended to look like an attack. It is made to cause a reaction that will open the line to which the real attack will be made, and it is made by extending the foil arm without moving the rest of the body. A feint may be made to any line, so you may

Fig. 2.29 Feint to the Open Line of Four.

feint a straight thrust, feint a disengage, or feint a cutover. The feint must be fast and decisively made, or it will not fool the opponent into thinking it is the real attack.

Beat. This is similar to a beat parry except that as an offensive action the beat is made with the foible against the foible. It is made with a clean, sharp, spanking action to either side of the blade. The beat may be very strong to open the line to be hit, or it may be a light beat to cause an answering beat from the opponent, thereby opening the opposite line for a disengage attack. The beat must be made close to the blade with no backswing or follow-through that would expose your own target.

Fig. 2.30   Beat in Preparation of Attack. (Photo by Robert Stadd)

Press. The press is similar to the beat but is a more subtle action. The fingers grip the handle forcefully to push, or press, the other blade. There should be no arm or hand motion, and the point must not move out of line but must be kept under control for the action that is to follow. Usually this is done to cause the opponent to press in return, and may be followed by a disengage or cutover.

Glide. This motion consists of gliding the blade along that of the opponent as the arm extends. It is similar to the feint and is useful against a light hand.

Derobement, or **Deceiving a Parry.** As the opponent attempts to parry your blade in answer to a beat, you may drop your point just low enough for the parry to pass over your blade without hitting it and then attack.

Some Examples of Compound Attacks   By combining one or more preparatory actions before the final thrust, you can make a wide variety of compound attacks.

One-Two. Feint a disengage to an unprotected line. If your opponent attempts a direct parry, deceive the parry with a disengage and lunge to score.

Can you distinguish feints from real attacks? Ask your partner to attack after a variable number of feints. Can you hold your parry until the real attack?

Double. Feint a disengage, just as for the one-two, but if a counter parry instead of a direct parry is made against the feint, deceive the counter parry by making a circle around the parry. In this attack there is no change of direction as the point disengages; then continues in the same direction as it began until it completes a full circle and one-half to land in the line first threatened by the feint. This may be described as a corkscrew attack.

Feint a Straight Thrust, Disengage. Much fencing is done in the guard of six with no blade contact. In this case a simple feint without changing line may force a parry that can be avoided, whether it is a direct or counter parry.

Defense Against Feint Attacks. When an attacker successfully deceives your parry of his feint, you must make a second parry. You may, for instance, try to parry a feint to the high-inside line with a parry of four, then parry a deceiving disengage with either a parry of counter four or direct six. It is a mistake to parry too quickly because this aids an attacker who wishes to make a one-two or double attack. It is better to wait until the attacker is fairly deep to parry.

Other Compound Attacks. There are numerous other compound attacks. For example, you can beat, or press, and straight thrust, disengage, or cutover; beat in the opposite line and straight thrust, cutover, or disengage; or feint any simple attack and disengage.

Attacks usually should not consist of more than two or three movements because an attack that takes too long to execute may be stopped before its completion by a counteraction from your opponent. Often the simplest attacks, made with great speed and accuracy at just the right time, are the most effective ones.

Attacks in Advance. When you fence out of distance, or when you feel certain that your opponent will retreat out of distance as you advance, you may advantageously make an advance attack to get within scoring distance. The shorter fencer must master this particular kind of attack in order to compensate for his shorter lunging distance. Any compound attack of two or three actions can be made in advance effectively. The feint, beat, or press is made as you advance; the final thrust is made as you lunge. For example, the one-two attack in advance is made by feinting a disengage while advancing and then making the final disengage while lunging.

Practice Drills

Working with a partner, designate one fencer as the attacker. The attacker makes a feint to any line, and the defender attempts to parry it. At first agree to use either direct or counter parries. The attacker tries to deceive the parry with a disengage lunge. After several attacks, the attacker becomes the defender so that the other fencer may attack. As the skill of each partner increases, the defender may parry with direct or counter parries, and the attacker may attempt to deceive them, but this is very difficult.

Later, the attacker may make an advance attack as the defender retreats and parries. Some attacks should be allowed to reach, and some should be parried by making a second parry. If a feint attack is correctly timed, there should not be any blade contact. If, on the other hand, the blade is clearly met by the defender during the feint, the attack has failed.

Common Faults

1. Lunging too soon. This causes the attacker's arm to withdraw during the attack, and he thereby loses right-of-way. Lunge when you are ready to score, not during your preparation.
2. Attacking from too far away. You must know you will reach your target.
3. Lack of confidence in an attack. If you doubt the success of an attack, there will be a tendency to withdraw the sword arm to parry before the attack is completed. Be sure of an attack or do not begin it. Confidence comes from repeated trials with full intent to score. Use attacks in practice until you can make them work.
4. Failure to feint convincingly. The feint must look like an attack, which means that you must extend your arm reach toward a threatened target rather than simply make a bent-arm feint to open air.
5. Overlunging, which causes a fencer to lose control and the ability to recover quickly to the guard position. Be sure of your distance before attacking, and never try to reach beyond the point of control.

SUGGESTED REFERENCES

CASTELLO, HUGO, and CASTELLO, JAMES. *Fencing.* New York: Ronald Press Co., 1962.
GARRET, MAXWELL R., and HEINECKE, MARY. *Fencing.* Boston: Allyn and Bacon, 1971.
PALFFY-ALPAR, JULIUS. *Sword and Masque.* Philadelphia: F. A. Davis Co., 1967.

Techniques for the
better fencer

3

When you have acquired ability to perform basic techniques, you can progress to more advanced techniques that will provide greater variety for your game.

ADVANCED FOOTWORK

The *pattinando* is a very fast advance-lunge. It begins by lifting the forward foot and then quickly hopping forward with the rear foot so that the feet land at almost the same time. The foil arm extends as the pattinando begins. The back foot should land about where the forward foot was before moving. This quick hop-advance is followed by a lunge, using the front toes to add impetus to the lunge as they hit the floor on the advance. There should be little upward motion as the fencer skims the surface of the strip.

The pattinando is invaluable against an out-of-distance or retreating fencer.

The *ballestra* is similar to the pattinando, but the feet land at the same time so there are only two sounds, that of the jump and that of the lunge. It may be described as a jump-lunge. The ballestra lends itself to two-part attacks, such as a one-two or any similar action.

The *fléche*, or running attack, is an advanced skill that can be used effectively but should be used sparingly. It is a swift attack which must be made very suddenly with no telegraphing motion so that it will surprise the opponent. It can be described as a do-or-die attack since it is an all-out attack in which the attacker runs past the other fencer as he attempts to score. To do this, he extends his arm as he drives his body forward with the right toe, then leads forward with the left foot, which passes beyond the right foot and continues running past his opponent. The attacker must run past, never into, the other fencer, for this could be dangerous to both fencers and is clearly forbidden in the rules of fencing. The attacker must allow his sword arm to relax with the hit to lessen the danger of breaking the blade. If this attack fails, the attacker may not continue fencing because action must stop as soon as one fencer passes another, although the defender may make an immediate riposte as the attacker runs past.

The flèche should not be made from much more than fencing distance. As the body moves forward in a near horizontal plane, the hit should arrive before taking the second step. A longer running attack is easily defended against. This is not a substitute for the lunge as some lazy fencers tend to believe, but a separate tactic that should be saved for special moments.

The flèche should never be made against an opponent who is inclined to stop thrust or advance into an attack. It is best made against an opponent who likes to retreat. It should not be used often since its main advantage lies in suprise, and since the attacker is unable to stop or change direction once the attack has begun.

Fig. 3.1 Fléche, or Running Attack. (Photo by Ric Thompson)

ATTACKS TO THE BLADE

Any action that deflects the opponent's blade from the target, thereby clearing the way for an attack, is an attack to the blade. The beat and press were discussed in chapter 2, but there are two additional attacks to the blade that should be mentioned. The *bind* and the *croise* are very useful actions that remove a menacing point and, if properly done, continue into a score.

The *bind* is made only against an extended arm with a menacing point. The extended arm should be fairly rigid so that the opponent's entire arm

---

When you make a bind, how does the action of your blade differ for an engagement in four and one in six?

---

and sword act as a lever. This action carries the blade from high line to low line, where the attacker attempts to score with a hit made in opposition to the blade, thereby assuring the attacker protection during this action. To make a bind, the attacker meets the foible of the opponent's blade with the forte of his own in four or six. If it is met in four, the point is guided over the opponent's blade and downward to score as the extending arm and hand moves to eight. From an engagement of sixth, the blade would pass over and downward to the position of seven. This must be very quickly done in one strong motion so that the other blade will be controlled throughout the attack.

This action, if very powerfully executed, can be used successfully to disarm an opponent, but there is no longer any advantage in doing so because action stops when a foil is dropped.

The defense against the bind consists of bending the foil arm to parry in seven or eight, depending on which side the attack is arriving. If the attacker is not quick enough or telegraphs his intent, it is not difficult to evade the attempt to bind by passing the point underneath the would-be attacker's blade, arm still extended and point in line.

The *croise* is made in much the same way as the bind, but it is made against a straight-arm attack that brings the opponent's blade so close to the target that a complete bind is dangerous, for it brings the blade across the body. If the opponent is close, the croise is better because it moves the opponent's extended arm from four to seven so that the blade does not cross one's own target.

VARIATIONS OF THE ATTACK

Change of Tempo

The list of attacks discussed in chapter 2 need not be expanded, but these attacks may be varied more effectively by changing the timing used in their execution. In the one-two or double, for instance, you can make a definite, but slightly slower, longer feint than usual followed by a sudden burst of speed as you make the final disengage, thereby upsetting the timing of the defense. This principle can be effectively applied to any attack. The disengage may be explosively fast or a very subtle, sliding attack that is deceptively slow.

The *false attack* is similar to a feint and is used for the same reasons, but it is made with a partial or full lunge. It must look like an attack, but

What attack to the blade is B using?
Is he correct in choosing this technique
when A's arm is straight?
How can A defend himself?

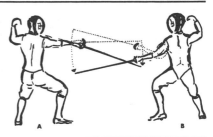

fall just short. It is done to provoke a response from the opponent which will, in turn, lead to the conclusion of the attack. Such an attack is often referred to as an "attack on second intent."

The false attack can be used against a person who often makes a stop thrust into your attack. With the false attack, the stop comes out, and the attacker then makes a quick parry of the stop and continues to hit. In this instance the arm must be withdrawn very little for the parry, and the parry must be very small so that the final attack will have only a few inches to travel before hitting; this short distance makes the false attack difficult to parry.

When you fence against a person who makes many second-intent attacks, the best defense is to retreat and make a decisive blocking parry.

COUNTER ATTACKS

Counter attacks are offensive actions made on attacks.

The *stop thrust* is a straight thrust, with or without a lunge, depending on the distance the thrust must travel to hit, into the opponent's attack or advance. It should be made only when the adversary withdraws his arm so that the stop arrives before the final action of the attack begins. If properly made, the stop will usually prevent the attack from hitting.

The stop is never a defense against a well-executed attack, but it takes right-of-way from an imperfect attack in certain instances. As long as an attack, even an imperfect one, continues in a forward direction, it may be considered right unless there is a definite withdrawal or hesitation of the sword arm between actions of a composed attack. It should be used sparingly since the attack almost always has right-of-way over a stop thrust. In the case of a double hit the decision as to who is right rests with the director, who may understandably have difficulty in accurately analyzing confusing actions.

The *stop with opposition* is similar to the stop thrust but is safer because the thrust is made with opposition which closes the line of attack. The stop with opposition is usually made against a compound attack. It should be timed so that the thrust is made during the final thrust of a one-two or a double. If the thrust is to the sixth line, a simple extension with opposition should be made to the opponent's right shoulder. If the thrust is to the fourth line, the extension should be made with opposition in eighth.

RIPOSTE

The riposte is a return attack made by a fencer who has parried an attack. The riposte may be simple or compound and may be made to any line. It may be made with a lunge if the opponent recovers to his guard position quickly, or it may be made by thrusting without a lunge if it is made quickly enough to arrive before the opponent has had time to recover.

An *immediate riposte* rebounds from the parry to score with a very fast direct thrust.

A *delayed riposte* is made after momentarily holding the parry, usually to riposte with a disengage or cutover that is made as the opponent's arm returns to the guard position. The riposte may be made with compound attacks, but often these are very time-consuming so that, except to surprise the opponent by changing tactics, the simple ripostes tend to be more successful.

A *counter riposte* may be made in just the same way by the fencer who has successfully parried a riposte.

Common Errors

1. Moving too close to the attacker, making it difficult to aim for a riposte.
2. Hesitating momentarily when making a direct riposte. A direct riposte should rebound from the parry to the target.
3. Extending the arm before aiming. Aim, extend, and then touch.

Fig. 3.2 Riposte—after the attacker's blade was parried. (Photo by Robert Stadd)

Estimate your maximum lunging distance and then test your judgment.
Can you barely hit the target from the starting position you chose?
As an opponent makes a simple attack, can you retreat just far enough
so that the attack lands short by 4 or 5 inches? by 1 or 2 inches?

THE REMISE

The remise is an offensive action made by the attacker who has failed to
hit on his first attempt. It is a second action that places the point on the
target without changing line and without withdrawing the arm. The remise
may be made when the opponent parries but does not riposte, or when
the riposte is delayed or composed. In order to maintain right-of-way, it
must start before the final action of the riposte, if any, begins.

When one fences a person who effectively uses the remise, immediate
simple ripostes are best because such ripostes have the legal right-of-way
over a remise, whereas a delayed or compound riposte does not. On the
other hand, when an opponent usually returns to the guard position after
his attack has been parried, the delayed or compound riposte may be more
effective.

FENCING WITH THE ELECTRIC FOIL

Since fencing is a combat sport, it is natural that participants should seek
competition with others once they have learned to effectively use the basic
skills. Because most competitive fencing has been electrically scored since
the 1955 World Championships, a word should be said about fencing with
the electrical foil.

The electric scoring apparatus is designed to determine hits made on
a fencer more accurately than the average judge can. The fencer's personal

Fig. 3.3 Fencing with the
Electric Foil—A. Scoring Ma-
chine; B. Reels; C. Reel
Wires. (Photo by Robert
Stadd)

equipment consists of an electric foil, a body cord, a jacket, an underarm protector, and a lamé vest which exactly covers the valid target and is worn over the regular fencing jacket.

The electric foil has a special point mounted on the end of the blade. The point is separated from its base by a spring that is depressed when a direct hit is made, causing the scoring apparatus to register a hit, valid or invalid. A thin wire is connected to the point and runs down the length of the blade, where it is embedded in a groove on the top of the blade to a plug on the inside of the guard. One end of the body cord plugs into the weapon, and the other connects with the signaling apparatus.

The signaling machine is equipped with a buzzer, which gives an auditory signal for a hit and two lights for each fencer. Whenever the lamé vest is hit, either a red or green light flashes, depending on which fencer has scored. If a hit arrives off target, it is indicated by a white light.

Anyone who intends to fence competitively should practice with an electric foil or with a dummy electric blade, which feels like an electric weapon but is less expensive for everyday use.

The first electric weapons were much heavier than the standard or non-electric foil. Consequently, point control was seriously affected, and for awhile it seemed that the methods of attack and defense would have to be modified. Weapons have been improved, however, so that, while there is still a difference in weight, the standard techniques are nonetheless correct. The difference is in the feel of the blade, which tends to be a little point-heavy. The point tends to whip more, which means that control is even more important than with the standard foil. A wide parry with the electric foil will travel farther and take longer to correct than when executed with a standard foil, so more precision is required. When using a standard foil, it is best to parry with the forte, or stronger part of the blade. An electric blade has more weight near the point than a standard one, and parries may be made nearer the center of the blade. This is advantageous because there will be less lateral whipping of the point when impact against the other blade occurs somewhat nearer the tip; therefore, controlling the point will be a little easier.

Fencers used to keep their points at eye level to provide a strong defense but with the heavier point, the chin-high guard previously described is preferred by most people, for it makes for greater accuracy and speed in the attack or riposte.

The electric foil has made touches to the eighth (low-outside) line very effective, for some fencers have difficulty in defending this line. If a defender lifts the elbow to parry in eight, a common fault, that line is further opened, and chances of deceiving that parry are also increased.

Have you compiled a mental list of the technique adjustments that should be made when fencing with an electric foil?

Low-line attacks are often frustrating in standard foil when judges call the touches because touches to the back are often obscured from their line of vision and go unnoticed.

To register a touch, the electric foil must arrive so that more than 500 grams of pressure are exerted on the tip. Before every competition and sometimes every bout, the foil should be tested by placing a 500-gram test weight, designed for this purpose, on the tip of the vertical foil. The tip should not be depressed until a light tap activates the circuit, after which the spring inside it should return the tip to its extended position. Fencers need not hit hard enough to bend the blade very much, and the hit need not remain on the target for the benefit of judges, so the attacker can, and should, be prepared to quickly go to the defense if necessary after touching, or to hit again immediately if there is no immediate riposte. Some fencers have a tendency to stop and look at the scoring machine when a point should have landed, but unless the point lands squarely (a point might land slightly sideways, or the fencers may be too close and bend the blade too much so that the pressure is on the edge of the tip), the machine will not register a touch, and the fencer who stops to look at the machine may be scored against easily if the previous touch did not activate it. For this reason, a fencer should keep fencing until the director halts the bout, so a quick remise is preferable to stopping to wait for a halt. Obviously, proper distance is very important.

Infighting, in which fencers inadvertently get very close, is allowed, provided that foils can still be used and that body contact does not occur. While this is not pretty fencing, it does occur, and some time should be spent in practicing touching and defending at close quarters.

SUGGESTED REFERENCES

CASTELLO, HUGO, and CASTELLO, JAMES. *Fencing*. New York: Ronald Press Co., 1962.

GARRET, MAXWELL R., and HEINECKE, MARY. *Fencing*. Boston: Allyn and Bacon, 1971.

PALFFY-ALPAR, JULIUS. *Sword and Masque*. Philadelphia: F. A. Davis Co., 1967.

How to improve your skills

4

The person who wishes to excel in any sport must spend countless hours in practice. This holds particularly true for fencing. Improper practice can be detrimental if poor offensive and defensive actions are allowed to become habit patterns, so practice sessions should always aim toward improving specific techniques. The fencer, whether beginning or experienced, must practice carefully and extensively in order to increase speed and accuracy of movements, endurance and strength, timing, and ability to respond quickly and with versatility.

WARMING UP

The value of warm-up exercises is that they reduce the possibility of injury, get a person mentally ready to perform, and serve to some degree as practice for what is to follow. To reduce the possibility of injury, slow, long, deep lunges probably serve as well as any other exercise because they will stretch the legs, groin, and torso areas—which are used strenuously in fencing. Once these areas are loosened through stretching, lunges should be increased in speed so that the whole warm-up period will serve as practice for fencing.

IMPROVING SPEED AND ACCURACY

To improve speed and accuracy of movement so that instantaneous responses to sudden actions will be well executed, rather than large and un-

On the wall, draw a three-inch circle within each of the four areas of an imaginary target. On twenty consecutive full-speed lunges can you hit a different circle each time? Can you do this after starting with a retreat-advance-lunge?

controlled, the fencer must concentrate on perfecting actions, and he must repeat them again and again until perfect motions are automatic. Although you often will react to a sudden threat on a subcortical level, you will just as often choose your actions, and you should have to decide only which movement to make, not how to execute it. The *how* must be made automatic through repetition.

To gain maximum improvement, the fencer should practice speed and accuracy of a skill simultaneously. In order to establish exactly how a motion should be made, an action may be practiced in slow motion, but once an action is understood, it should be practiced at full but controlled speed. This will develop speed as well as accuracy.

The lunge, for instance, must be performed powerfully if a fencer is practicing to attack more effectively. Once you have lunged at full speed, stay in the lunge position long enough to make sure that all parts of your body are correctly aligned. If they are not, correct your position and repeat the lunge again and again until you are satisfied that it is well executed. When you reach this point, practice an immediate recovery from the full lunge to the guard position. You may then progress to the advance-lunge, recover, retreat, and so forth, all of which can be practiced in the same manner.

A padded target can be hung on a wall so that you can practice point control and proper thrusting along with footwork. If you lunge to hit a target, try to hit as near a specific spot as you can. At the same time, practice to increase your ability to judge fencing distance accurately. From how far away can you lunge and hit? How far away from the target should you be to hit with an advance lunge or ballestra attack?

Footwork can be practiced most effectively by yourself or with a capable person watching and correcting you; do not try to perfect your basic form as you fence when your mind must be occupied with many other things.

PRACTICING WITH ANOTHER FENCER

In order to make your practice time profitable, you should practice specific skills with another person. This can be interesting, and challenging, and will improve your technique more quickly than free play.

Alternative Exercises

Any attack and defense can be practiced by having one person make attacks while the other parries. For example, one fencer may make disengage or one-two attacks while the other parries with only counter parries or only direct parries. Any technique can be practiced in this way with the attacker trying to increase his or her speed and accuracy. The attacker must try to land each time in order to challenge the defender. The defender occasionally should allow an attack to land to make sure that it is being made well. Trade off so that each partner works at attack and defense.

As soon as this simple exercise is mastered, progress by adding a riposte which may or may not be parried. More interest may later be stimulated by allowing the attacker to make any attack and the defender to make any defense and riposte. The partner system also should be used to practice the advance-lunge as the defender retreats and then parries and ripostes with a lunge if necessary.

BOUTING PRACTICE

Only after much drilling should you progress to actual bouting. Even bouting will be more advantageous if you try to use those skills you have previously practiced in a bout situation so that you can see what you still have to improve, and so that you can gain confidence in your ability to execute various techniques successfully. While you bout, you should try to analyze how each point that scored against you was made and what you could do to prevent it in the future. It is just as important to know exactly how you scored when you were successful in attacking. During actual competition you will need to be fully confident of certain offensive actions because confidence is a necessary ingredient in successful fencing. It also is important to fence with as many different people as you can since you tend to become stereotyped when you fence with only one person and get to know his or her every move. Of course you will profit most from working with fencers who are better than you are. More skilled fencers are obligated to spend some time with the less skilled. This should not be an excessive amount of time because such practice may work to the disadvantage of the better fencer. The highly skilled fencer may profit from working with beginners if he practices for greater precision in spite of his opponent's larger motions because he may have more time to work on distance judgment or to experiment with new ideas. Sometimes there is a tendency to make wide motions against a fencer who does the same, but this should always be avoided. Fence your best, no matter who your partner is.

Increasing Endurance

The strength-endurance factor is a requirement for today's fencer and can be increased in many ways. You can lunge 100 or more times a day, working until you are tired. This will increase endurance and also provide practice in lunging. Running will increase overall stamina and, to a degree, leg strength. Running up stairs, preferably two stairs at a time, will increase endurance and leg strength more than straight running will. You also may practice fencing for increasingly longer periods of time, working until you are fatigued.

Whatever method you choose, you must be in top physical condition to be a competitive fencer. College fencing tournaments frequently last for twelve or more hours during which time the contestants fence a bout, rest for from two to twenty minutes, fence again, rest again, and so forth. Strength and endurance are necessary if participants are to keep fencing effectively for such an extended period. Because fencing is a very mobile game with many running attacks or attacks in advance, it is extremely taxing, even for one hard-fought bout, and the fencer who is in poor physical condition will not be able to maintain his highest level of efficiency.

SUGGESTED REFERENCES

CASTELLO, HUGO, and CASTELLO, JAMES. *Fencing.* New York: Ronald Press Co., 1962.

GARRET, MAXWELL R., and HEINECKE, MARY. *Fencing.* Boston: Allyn and Bacon, 1971.

SIMONIAN, CHARLES. *Fencing Fundamentals.* Columbus, Ohio: Charles E. Merrill Publishing Co., 1968.

The bout

5

The bout is much like a two-way conversation—either person may initiate the action, the other responds in turn, and they continue to interact. Occasionally both may take the initiative at the same time, but usually it is a give-and-take situation.

The rules of fencing give precedence, or right-of-way, to the one who first seizes the initiative with an arm extension or an attack. The attacker loses right-of-way when the attack is parried or fails, or if he or she withdraws the arm during the attack. Once the attack or feint is deflected, the defender has the right-of-way to riposte if he or she immediately seizes it. If there is a delay, neither party has right-of-way, and it may be retaken by either fencer.

When your technique has progressed sufficiently, you will want to test your ability against another fencer in a bout situation. Bouting is a true test of your speed, power, timing, ability to control your emotions and body; of your ability to analyze another fencer; and of your ingenuity. You are completely on your own, and you will win or lose depending on how well you apply your knowledge. You often will need to make split-second decisions and decisively carry them out.

Whether you are engaged in informal bouting practice or in a tournament, you must try to score with the same determination, or you will do a disservice to yourself and to your opponent. Neither of you will benefit from half-hearted attempts to attack or defend. In a practice bout, however, you are more free to experiment and to use attacks and defenses that you have been practicing. In competitive fencing you must use actions in which you have gained confidence during practice sessions. The harder you have worked, and the more you have experimented in practice bouting, the more choice of action you will have to select from in a tournament situation.

The main problem in bouting with another person is deciding what to do and when to do it. This chapter is devoted to attempting to answer these questions. In a contest between two otherwise evenly matched fencers, the bout will go to the one who more effectively outthinks the other. You must always be aware of your own responses to probing actions made by your opponent. You should try not to respond to feints unless you choose to invite an attack in order to set up an action for yourself, and you must avoid any repetitious actions such as a continual change of engagement in advance or patterns of beating without a definite plan in mind. Be aware of every move you make, know why you make it, and watch your opponent's reactions to what he learns about you.

TESTING FOR REACTIONS

The first thing you will probably do when you face another fencer is to test his responses. You must find out how fast he moves, how large or small his actions are, how he tends to react, what kinds of traps he will fall into, and what kinds he will lay for you. If you fence against a person you know very well, you must still learn how he feels and how fast he is today.

There are a number of ways to discover what you want to know so that you can plan your tactics according to what the other person is likely to do. This preliminary testing must be sudden and convincing to draw a true response from your opponent, who is probably trying to find out the same things about you.

Responses to a Feint or False Attack

There are several responses you can draw from a feint or false attack:

1. A parry response, with or without a riposte, means that a one-two or double, depending on whether a direct or counter parry was used, will be a logical choice of attacks.

2. If a strong feint brings no response at all, your opponent is probably well controlled and will not parry until he is certain that you intend to hit with a direct attack. In this instance, try an explosive direct attack to score. If it succeeds, try the same thing again until it fails. If it is parried, how did your opponent parry it? You are again ready for a one-two or double, but it will be more difficult to time against a de-

layed parry. You will need a deep feint with a last-minute evasion of the parry.

3. A retreat with or without a parry may indicate that an advance attack will be necessary for your proposed attack to reach. Plan an advance attack that will deceive any defensive attempts.

4. An extension into your feint tells you that you can expect your opponent to make stop thrusts. You can precede a straight thrust or disengage with a beat to either side of the blade to gain clear right-of-way. You can also effectively make a second-intent attack in which you make a false attack, parry the stop, and continue to hit.

Responses to a Beat or Press

You can beat lightly on either side of the blade or press in the line of engagement to discover how your opponent reacts. He may:

1. Make an answering beat or press, in which case you may beat or press and make a disengage or a one-two, timing the feint, or disengage so that the answering beat or press will not find your blade and the opponent will be forced to go for a parry. If you are faster than he is, a disengage may work, but if he parries well, a one-two will be better. You have set up a lateral movement with your preliminary action.

2. Make no response, which means that a strong beat-straight thrust may score. After being hit in this manner, the opponent will parry a strong feint of a straight thrust so that you can set up your deceptive attacks.

3. Attack as you beat or press. You can then "invite" him to attack by making a beat or press and then, since you are expecting the attack and will be ready, parry and riposte.

Responses to a Change of Engagement

With or without an advance, a change of engagement may reveal something about your opponent. He may:

1. Change his hand position to protect the line to which you have changed. You may change engagement and then make a disengage or one-two as your opponent's hand moves to protect the line to which you have moved; again, this will set up a lateral response on the part of the other fencer. You can vary this action by making the attack to his low line.

2. Change engagement to the original line. You may change, then make a derobement, which is a disengage that avoids an opponent's change.

If the opponent parries this, avoid by disengaging again to the high or low line.

3. Make a disengage attack. Any time you change, you must be ready to parry a possible derobement against you and then riposte. The fact that you are prepared for this possible attack gives you an advantage. A counter parry may be more effective than a direct parry because your opponent is more likely to try a one-two than a double in the event of a parry.

4. Not respond at all, in which case you may change, feint a glide to force a response, and deceive the parry. Caution is always necessary against someone who does not react to tentative maneuvers. He is probably planning to use such preliminary motions against you in the near future, so use variety and never set up a pattern of changing or beating unless you intend to invite an attack.

Responses to Simple Attacks or Beat Attacks

Often a sudden, explosive, unexpected attack can be enough of a surprise to be successful. If this works, try it again until it fails; then you will be ready for a composed attack to avoid whatever parry has been used to block the attack.

VARYING YOUR DISTANCE

You should move about on the strip. If you freeze in one place on the strip, you allow two things to happen: first, you allow your opponent too much time to get set for an attack; second, you tend to lessen your ability to move quickly and powerfully. As you move you can keep yourself ready to attack at all times. Any time you advance to within fencing distance, your opponent may attack and catch you slightly off-balance and moving into the attack. To avoid this you should either extend your arm, beat-extend, or otherwise control the opponent's blade as you advance; however, you must change what you do as you advance to lessen the likelihood of having your actions anticipated. Never simply advance into a hit.

On the other hand, as you advance and retreat to varying distances, you should try to draw your opponent a little too close. You must be completely alert so that you can attack at the exact instant he raises his toes to make an advance that will bring him within lunging distance and allow you to make an attack that, from previous preliminary movements, you are sure will land.

As a rule, you should retreat as you parry to add an extra margin of safety and to allow more time for your defense. If you retreat too far, how-

---

---

ever, you cannot riposte. Through experience you will learn to retreat far enough so that your opponent's attack lands just short; then a half or full lunge with your riposte will be sufficient to reach.

ATTACKS ON PREPARATION

The best time to attack is while your opponent is preparing to attack, but before he actually begins. For instance, if you learn by observation that your opponent likes to make a beat or change in advance, you may make a disengage or a one-two that avoids his attempt to meet your blade as he steps in, or by making a bind, you may take the initiative from a feint. Absolute concentration and alertnesss are necessary if you are to time an attack on preparation successfully; however, this is a very exciting way to fence since the split-second timing required tends to keep you on your toes so that you can detect any movement of which you can take advantage.

BUILDING ATTACK SEQUENCES

Although it has been mentioned briefly, the possibility of progressing from simple to complex actions deserves special emphasis. To the degree that your opponent allows, you can lead him through a number of attacks and continue to build on his defensive responses to previous attacks.

You first may make a straight thrust, beat-straight thrust, disengage, or beat-disengage attack. Try to score; if you do, continue this attack until, in essence, you teach your opponent to parry it. You may advance, retreat, feint, or change engagement between attacks to divert your opponent's attention from your strategy. If you desire a direct parry to your direct attack, you are more likely to get it by attacking away from the other blade rather than with opposition because a counter parry is more difficult when it must be moderately wide. If your attack fails because your opponent, now convinced that you will continue to make simple attacks, parries with a direct parry, you can follow this up with a one-two attack. The one-two may be used, interspersed with diverting byplay, until it is parried with a second parry; then you may make the one-two by making the last action to the low line.

If your opponent switches to counter parries, you may similarly progress to double attacks.

Another sequence of attacks may begin with a cutover from the line of four to an open line of six. If you are engaged in four, you may make a simple cutover or a press cutover that may open the sixth line further if your opponent responds to the press with pressure of his own. If you begin in six, you may change engagement to four and make the cutover as your opponent starts to close his fourth line. This is an effective attack and should land. When this is parried by a direct parry of six, you may, on the next attack feint a cutover and avoid the sixth parry to disengage low to eighth. When this attack is parried, you may progress to a feint of a cutover to eighth and disengage to sixth.

There will be other byplay between attacks—you may keep the offensive by controlling the blade or changing distance, or you may go to the defense yourself. The time you pick to attack is important. The distance must be right, and you must catch your opponent as he relaxes a little or as his attention wanders momentarily. You must surprise him.

You may devise progressions of your own in this manner. One effective variation of this concept is to make a simple attack, then a two-part attack that changes line, and, finally, return to the first simple action when your second action is parried. The defender will be expecting your second action and will react little, if at all, to your feint; when this happens, turn the feint into the attack. It has been said that if all of a fencer's feints looked like attacks and all attacks looked like feints, you could always be a winner.

THE LEFT-HANDED FENCER

Those fencers who are left-handed may have a psychological advantage over some opponents, and they will have a technical advantage over those who are unfamiliar with left-handed fencers. Right-handed fencers should fence with left-handers often to familiarize themselves with the differences that exist between left- and right-handed fencing.

Left-handers must develop a strong defense in the outside lines since this will be their most vulnerable area. When fencing a right-hander, they will be in six, often a weaker line, when the right-hander is in the stronger line of four, and vice versa. A strong parry of six, counter six, and eight are important for both left- and right-handed fencers when they work against one another.

Very few inside attacks will succeed in this situation, but a one-two to the inside and then to the outside or low line is an effective attack for either fencer. Accuracy is important here since the outside lines are smaller than those on the inside; however, they are more accessible.

Attacks on preparation may be effective if either fencer insists on engaging in either six or four. The attacker may change to the nonfavored line and make a derobement as the other fencer changes back to his preferred line.

SUGGESTED COUNTERS TO COMMON SYSTEMS OF FENCING

There are many possible ways of dealing with various strategies. The important thing is to recognize a style for what it is and plan to use this knowledge to your own advantage. The following represent possible means of solving some common problems which you may encounter:

1. Against a fencer who makes many stop or counter thrusts you may succeed with second-intent attacks.

2. Against an opponent who refuses to attack, but who has a deadly parry riposte, you also may be successful with a second-thrust attack that will bring about the desired attack for your parry and counter riposte.

3. Against a fencer who is always out of reach, you may make a pattinando or ballestra attack, you may redouble to pursue the opponent, or you may retreat yourself to attack as he advances into distance.

4. Against a fencer who wants to control your blade and who makes many beat attacks, you may fence with absence of the blade. If you take a low-line guard, your opponent will be frustrated in his attempt to take your blade. If he goes to a low line to find your blade, which is a fairly large action, you may take the initiative with a derobement to the high line. You may pretend to give him your blade and disengage as soon as he moves to find your blade.

5. Against a person who always makes an advance attack or ballestra, you may upset the distance by occasionally holding your ground rather than retreating. Since this moving attack is calculated to reach a retreating defender, by holding your ground your attacker will not have reached the final phase of his attack by the time the distance to your target is closed, and his point will probably miss because he will not be ready for the final thrust in time. The riposte after your parry will not be difficult because you know what the distance will be and can thrust accordingly.

6. Against bent-arm simple attacks, a stop thrust with opposition is effective. Against a poor compound attack, a stop thrust made before the final action begins can take the right-of-way.

HINTS FOR THE DEFENSE

Control is the watchword for the defender. You should watch the center of the target. You should not try to watch the point as it moves, for it will move too wide and too fast for the eye to follow. Nor should you try to follow movement of the hand with your eyes. If you watch a central point on the target, you will be able to see everything that develops

How might fencer B safely attack fencer A?

with your peripheral vision. You will see any shoulder movements that may telegraph an attack, you will see where the hand moves, and you will be able to see foot movements without having to follow all of these movements with your eye.

Try to parry only the real attacks, not the feints. The ability to tell a feint from an attack is acquired through experience, but the beginner can refuse to parry until the lunge actually develops. By delaying the parry, you give your opponent fewer clues, and you make compound attacks difficult to time. Ideally, you should parry just before the point lands, which takes a good eye, control, and precision in the parry.

Be sure to use variety in your defense, particularly against an experienced fencer. Mix the use of four and six and of direct and counter parries so that an attacker will have a difficult time accurately anticipating your defense. Avoid falling into a set pattern for your defense unless you do it deliberately to entrap your opponent. It is virtually impossible to be flexible enough to react with a different action the instant an attack is launched against you, but once you have reacted to a parry, ask yourself what parry it was, and then plan how you will react to the next attack. You can program yourself to react in a certain way—you may take a second direct parry, a counter on the third, and continue to vary your responses.

Defense against a Riposte

Once you have initiated an attack, you must try to follow it to a successful touch, but if you hear or feel the steel of your opponent's blade as it parries yours, you must immediately go to your defense. Since a parry involves only the sword arm and blade, it can be made even if you are in the act of lunging or in a full lunge and cannot immediately return to the guard position. It is a mistake to feel you cannot defend until your body is out of the way because the arm and sword can move instantly if the elbow is not locked. It is difficult to establish this reaction, but with much practice it can become a reflex action. Against a good fencer who may do something other than make a direct riposte, a safe defense is to quickly parry in four and six or four-six-four, so you can find the blade wherever it is.

SUGGESTED REFERENCES

CASTELLO, HUGO, and CASTELLO, JAMES. *Fencing.* New York: Ronald Press Co., 1962.

CROSNIER, ROGER. *Fencing with the Electric Foil.* New York: A. S. Barnes and Co., 1961.

GARRET, MAXWELL, R., and HEINECKE, MARY. *Fencing.* Boston: Allyn and Bacon, 1971.

PALFFY-ALPAR, JULIUS. *Sword and Masque.* Philadelphia: F. A. Davis Co., 1967.

Rules of fencing

6

Fencing rules are established by the Federation Internationale d'Escrime (FIE), the governing body of international fencing. These current rules, translated from French into English, were published in America through the cooperation of the Amateur Fencers League of America (AFLA) and the National Collegiate Athletic Association (NCAA). The publication includes FIE "Rules for Competitions," the AFLA operations manual, and the NCAA rules governing collegiate fencing.[1]

FIELD OF PLAY

The foil strip, or piste, may have a wood, rubber, linoleum, cork, or plastic surface. The strip is from 1.8 to 2 meters (5 feet 11 inches to 6 feet 7 inches) wide and 14 meters (46 feet) long. Seven lines should be drawn across the width of the strip: one center line; two on-guard lines, one drawn 2 meters

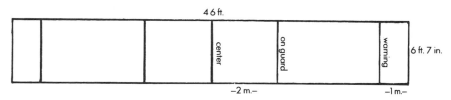

Fig. 6.1   The Foil Strip.

1. The manual may be purchased for $3.00 from: Amateur Fencers League of America, Inc., 33 62nd Street, West New York, N. J. 07093.

(6 feet 7 inches) from each side of the center line; two end lines at the rear limit of the strip; and two warning lines marked 1 meter (3 feet 3 inches) in front of the end lines.

CLOTHING

Fencers are responsible for their own safety. They must wear an all-white uniform that provides the maximum possible safety without sacrificing freedom of movement.

The jacket must overlap the trousers at the waist by at least four inches in the guard position. Fencers must wear an underarm protector in addition to the padded jacket, and women, especially in electrically scored events, are required to wear rigid breast protectors.

Men and women are required to wear trousers that fasten below the knee, which means they may be knickers or ankle-length pants. If knickers are worn, white stockings also must be worn so that no bare skin is exposed on the leg. College fencers are allowed to wear colored stockings in collegiate meets, and they often show their school colors in this manner.

The gauntlet of the glove must cover about half of the forearm to prevent the opponent's blade from entering the jacket sleeve.

MANNER OF FOIL FENCING

Fencers may fence in their own styles if they observe the rules of fencing. These rules require that fencers compete in a courteous and honest manner. Dangerous actions such as running into the opponent or otherwise fencing with lack of body control are forbidden. Fencers are required to keep their masks on until a decision has been rendered by the director during a bout.

Touching. The foil is a thrusting weapon only, and offensive actions must be made with the point, which must distinctly reach the target in order to be counted as a touch.

Target. The valid target for men and women is the torso from the collar to a horizontal line that joins the tops of the hip bones across the back, and to the groin line in front. The arms, from the shoulder seams outward, are excluded. The bib of the mask is also excluded.

Off-Target Hits. When a point touches any part of the body other than the target, it is not a valid touch, but it stops all action and no subsequent touch is allowed.

Handling the Weapon. The foil may be used with one hand only. A fencer may not switch hands during a bout unless the director gives special permission because of an injury.

Coming on Guard. The fencer whose name is called first should come on guard on the director's right, unless the first person called is a left-handed fencer, in which case he should go to the director's left.

Length of a Bout. A bout lasts until one person has been hit five times. If it is a timed meet, the time limits are six minutes of actual fencing time. College bouts, however, are four minutes long. Fencers may ask the score during a bout, but they may not ask how much time remains. If the time limit expires before the bout is completed, each fencer's score advances to meet the required number of points to win a bout. In a five-point bout, for instance, if time runs out when the score is 3-1, two points are added to each score to make the official score 5-3. If a bout is tied at the end of the fencing period, the score will be advanced to 4-4, and the fencers will continue, regardless of time, until the final point is won. Fencers receive a verbal warning from the director when one minute of time remains.

The fencers must start in the center of the width of the strip, with both feet behind their respective on-guard lines, which are 6 feet 7 inches from the center line.

At the command "On guard," the fencers come to the guard position. Then the director next asks, "Are you ready?" When both fencers reply in the affirmative, the director begins the bout with the command "Fence."

Beginning, Stopping, and Restarting the Bout. At the command "Fence," time is in, and either fencer may initiate the offensive. Once play begins, the contestants may stop only at their own risk until the bout is officially stopped by the command "Halt."

Only the director may halt the bout unless an unsafe situation arises; then a judge may halt the bout. If, for instance, a judge sees an injury or a broken blade, he may stop the bout.

The director stops the bout when a touch, valid or off target, is made, when a fencer steps off of the strip with both feet, anytime a corps à corps or any other irregular play exists, whenever a judge raises his hand, or when, in his opinion, the bout should be stopped for any other reason.

Fencing at Close Quarters. This is allowed as long as the fencers are able to use their weapons correctly and the director can follow the action.

Displacing the Target and Reversing Positions. Displacing the target, ducking, and turning are allowed, but reversing position or turning one's back to the opponent on the strip is not. If this occurs, fencers are halted and put on guard in their original positions.

Improper Use of the Unarmed Hand or Arm. Use of the unarmed hand or arm is not allowed nor may a fencer cover any part of the valid target with the unarmed hand or arm.

Penalty for this offense is loss of a touch, after a warning, if a touch were made during this action, or a touch against the offender if the other fencer did not score a valid touch in this action. However, a bout may not be lost on a penalty, so if a penalty touch would end the bout, one touch must be subtracted from the opponent's score.

Ground Gained or Lost. When the bout is halted, each fencer must retreat equally in order to maintain fencing distance. The following cases are exceptions to this rule: when a valid hit is scored, fencers are put on guard at equal distances from the center of the strip, as they were at the beginning of the bout; when a bout stops because of a corps-à-corps or fleche, only the fencer who caused the clinch must give ground; a competitor cannot be put on guard behind the warning line if he has not been previously warned; a fencer who was behind the warning line when the bout was stopped does not have to give ground.

Stepping Off of the Strip. Whenever a fencer steps off of the strip with both feet, the director must immediately call "Halt." If a fencer is touched as he steps off by an action that was already in motion as he stepped off the strip, the touch is awarded. Any touch made by a fencer who has stepped off of the strip must be annulled.

Rear Limits of the Strip. If a competitor's rear foot reaches the warning line, the director must halt the bout to warn him that he is nearing the end line. This warning is repeated each time the previously warned fencer advances so that his front foot reaches his on-guard line and retreats again to the warning line.

If a fencer crosses the rear line with both feet after a warning, a point is scored against him. If a fencer crosses the end line without having been warned, he is put on guard at the warning line with no penalty.

Lateral Boundaries. When a fencer crosses a side line with both feet he is penalized 1 meter (3 feet 3 inches). If this penalty places him over the end line with both feet, a touch will be awarded against him if he was warned previously at the warning line.

If a fencer crosses a boundary to avoid being hit, he is warned. The second time this occurs during the same bout, a touch is awarded against him. If a fencer accidentally leaves the strip, there is no penalty.

Corps-à-Corps and Flèche Attacks. When a fencer systematically causes a corps-a-corps, even without violence, he first is warned and then is penalized one hit for each repetition during the same bout.

OFFICIALS

The Director or President. The director is completely in charge of the bout over which he presides. His duties are to stop and start the bout, to make sure that all clothing and equipment is safe and legal, to supervise the other officials, to maintain order, to penalize for faults, and to award touches.

If one judge says "Off target," the other abstains, and the director believes the touch was valid, what is the decision on the touch?

The Jury. If a tournament is fenced with standard (nonelectric) weapons, the jury consists of a director and four judges. When the event is electrically scored, if there is no metallic strip, the jury may consist of two ground judges.

Duties of the Judges. Two judges stand on each side of the director, one on each side of the strip, slightly behind the fencers. Each judge watches the fencer who is farthest away from him, so that the two judges on the director's right watch the fencer on the director's left, and vice versa.

Judges watch for any hits, valid or not, that land on the fencer. When a point lands, the judge must immediately signal the director by raising his or her hand and the director must then call "Halt."

Method of Determining Hits

The director must briefly reconstruct the actions of the last phrase and ask the appropriate judges whether a hit was made in the course of play.

A judge may respond by saying "Yes," which means a valid hit was made; "Off target," which means a hit landed but was not valid; "No"; or "I abstain," which means that the judge did not see the action, which may have been blocked from his vision by one or both fencers, and declines to vote.

The director votes last and adds up the votes as follows: one point for the vote of each judge; one and one-half points for his own vote; and no points for an abstention. If two judges on one side agree that a touch was valid, off target, or did not land, their decision must stand, even if the director does not agree, because their two votes outweigh the director's one and one-half votes.

If, on the other hand, one judge says "No" and one says "Yes" or "Off target," the director has the deciding vote.

If one judge says "Yes," "Off target," or "No," and the other abstains, the director may overrule the judge who has voted if he does not agree with him.

If one judge answers "Yes" or "Off target," and the other answers "No," and if the director abstains, no point is awarded, but no subsequent action may be awarded against the fencer who might have landed a hit. If the fencer who made the doubtful touch then makes a definite touch without a touch having landed against him, the touch must be awarded.

The jury decides materiality of hits. Once materiality has been established, the director alone decides on the validity of a touch. In the event that two touches land at the same time, the director determines which, if either, fencer gets the point.

Ground Judges

When a meet is electrically scored but not fenced on a metal strip, two ground judges are needed. The judges stand on opposite sides of the director one at each end of the strip and observe all action. They determine whether a touch that registers as an off-target touch was made on the floor.

Scorer

The scorer marks points against the fencers when they are declared touched. He or she marks the hit and announces the name and score of the person who was scored against and then announces the score of the other fencer. The scorer also calls fencers to the strip to fence and announces "on deck" bouts so that the next two to fence will be ready when their turn comes and no time will be lost in starting the next bout.

Timer

In an official meet a time limit is set on bouts. The timer uses a stopwatch to keep track of actual fencing time only. Time is in from the director's command of "Fence" to that of "Halt." The timer signals the director, who must stop the bout and warn the fencers when only one minute of time remains. At the end of the final minute, the timer stops the bout by ringing a bell or buzzer or by calling "Halt."

OFFICIATING TECHNIQUES

At most fencing tournaments fencers are expected to be willing and able to assist with the officiating. Directors are, for the most part, amateur fencers who gladly give their time in the interest of fencing. It is desirable, therefore, that all fencers learn to officiate in any capacity so that they can assist in the running of meets and better understand and appreciate all aspects of the sport.

It takes experience to become a good director or judge. These tasks require the entire attention of officials involved if they are to see and explain accurately what occurs during a bout. The entire climate of a tournament is affected by the attitudes and abilities of the director and his jury,

GV
1147
B68   15,532
c.1

CAMROSE LUTHERAN COLLEGE
LIBRARY

who may either inspire confidence and establish a high level of efficiency or allow indecision and poor sportsmanship to lower the standards and morale of fencers and spectators alike.

Directing Techniques

The director is a vital part of a tournament. He or she is responsible for and has authority over the actions of both fencers and spectators. He or she sets the standard and overall climate of the meet.

The director must know the rules, but in case he is challenged or an unusual situation arises, he should have a rule book available. The director's voice should be clear and authoritative so that the commands of "Fence" and "Halt" may be heard clearly by both the fencers and the timer.

Starting the Bout   The director must see that the fencers and officials are all in place before beginning the bout. As soon as they are in place he asks, "Are you ready?", and when the fencers reply in the affirmative, he says, "Fence."

Directing with a Jury   Since standard foils must often be used in classroom tournaments, it is necessary that students understand how to be an effective official in such instances.

The director stands midway between the fencers and about ten feet to the side so that he can follow the action and still see the judges. As the action moves up and down the strip, he or she moves with the fencers at all times.

The director allows play to continue until a point lands or any irregular fencing occurs, or he feels it should be stopped for any reason.

A director can upset the fencers by calling halt too often for no reason. As long as no point has landed and the fencing is not too confusing to follow, competitors should be allowed to continue. However, if there is cause, the bout should be halted immediately. If several actions take place after a point lands, it is more difficult to analyze play, so the call to halt must be issued immediately after a point arrives.

When action stops because of a possible touch, the director should quickly give a résumé of the last phrase. The director is there to run a bout efficiently with a minimum of delays, not to put on an exhibition of his knowledge or to overshadow the fencing with his performance. He is only there to facilitate fencing, and lengthy explanations of every detail of the bout may unduly delay the game.

After a brief description of the last phrase, the director should ques-

These fencers have made valid touches at about the same time. Under what circumstances would you declare fencer A hit? fencer B hit?

tion the judges about the materiality of hits. He should follow the right-of-way sequence and determine whether the first attack landed. If it did and the right-of-way was clear, a point is awarded, and no further questions need to be asked. If the attack failed, he must find out which, if any, subsequent action landed and award hits according to his findings.

The director should always give his own opinion of materiality last so that he does not influence the responses of the judges in any way. He should not lead the judges with such questions as, "Did you see the point land on the hand?" or "Do you agree that the point missed?" It would be better to ask, "Did the attack land?" a simple statement that does not suggest how the judge should answer.

Validity   If both fencers are hit, the director alone is responsible for determining validity. He also may see points land, but first he must know the sequence of action. If two touches arrive at about the same time, he must decide which fencer had the right-of-way, and if he cannot, he must declare a simultaneous touch, in which case no touch is awarded.

Unfortunately, inconsistencies in determining right-of-way in competitive fencing are seen too often. It is important for a director to be consistent in deciding validity. Generally speaking, the attack is considered correct if two touches occur at about the same time. While a straight-arm attack is advantageous to the attacker, it is not mandatory from the director's standpoint. The sword arm should move forward before or during the attack, but it need not be fully extended to take right-of-way. For instance, a continuous one-two attack, even if it is imperfect, will not lose right-of-way to a stop thrust, unless the stop *arrives* before the last action *begins*.

When a halt is called and no touch is awarded, the director must indicate the center of the field of play so the fencers can properly position themselves when they are ready to resume action. Besides allowing the director to see the action clearly, this central position simplifies the task of indicating the center of the field of play and keeps the director out of the judges' line of vision.

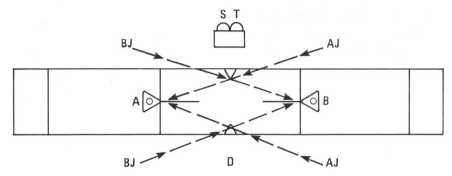

Fig. 6.2   Placement of Officials—Standard Foil with Judges. A. Fencer A;
AJ. Judges Who Watch Fencer A; B. Fencer B; BJ. Judges Who Watch Fencer
B; D. Director; S. Scorer; T. Timer.

Judging Techniques

Each judge watches materiality of touches against the fencer who is farthest
away from him. The judges are to assist the director and are not in any
way to try to dominate or delay the fencing.

A judge must move with the action to maintain his position just behind the nearest fencer and at the side of the strip. In this position judges
will not obstruct the view of the director or get in the way of the fencers,
yet at least one of the two judges at each end of the strip will have a clear
view of what happens. While the judges are not responsible for knowing who
has the right-of-way, they must know how many actions were made against
the fencer they are watching so that they will know which attempt touched
when there has been a series of actions. It is to a judge's advantage to count
actions as they occur so that he can say clearly whether it was the first, second, or fourth action that landed.

The judge must raise his hand instantly when he sees a point land, on
or off target. If he hesitates, it will be harder to decide which action landed
and time will be lost, so he must raise his hand quickly and high enough
to be seen clearly out of the corner of the director's eye. Conversely, he
must not raise his hand unless he sees something land. Nothing is more
annoying to a fencer who has planned a series of actions that he believes
will lead to a hit than to have a judge stop the action by raising his hand,
only to say, "No, I guess nothing really happened," or "I'm not sure."

When the director asks a judge whether an action landed or not, he
does not want a lengthy description of where and how the point went. The
judge's response should be: "Yes," "Off target," "No," or "Abstain." A good
judge abstains when he does not see whether a point landed or not; an
abstention simply may be a weak, indecisive answer from a judge who is

Fig. 6.3 Students Officiating a Standard Foil Bout. Raised hands indicate judges have seen both fencers touch. The director is polling the judges. (Photo by Robert Stadd)

afraid to express opinion for fear of being wrong. A judge must tell what he sees without being influenced by another judge's opinion or by comments or gestures from fencers or spectators. He must be sure of himself and answer to the best of his ability at all times, not just take the easy way out by refusing to vote.

Directing With Electrical Apparatus

The duties of the director are the same whether a meet is electrically scored or not, but the means of deciding touches is different. When there are no judges to assume partial responsibility, the director's task is perhaps even more demanding. Although the machine alone can determine if a point has been made, the director must be aware of all of the action which takes place, and he must also watch the scoring box so that he will see when a light goes on.

His first task, at the start of each bout, is to see that all equipment is working properly before fencing begins, even though fencers are responsible for their own personal equipment. If a foil is not registering properly or there are any tears in an electric vest, he must see that they are repaired or replaced.

Position   The director should stand so that he can see the scoring lights as well as the action at all times. This means that, except when fencers are in the center of the strip, the director will stand at one end of the action or the other so that he can see both the fencers and the lights. If lights of both fencers have turned on, he must still be aware of who has the right-of-way so that he can decide to whom to award a point.

How to Read the Lights   There are two lights for each fencer: a white light and a colored light. The bout must be stopped whenever a light and the buzzer go on. No touch may be awarded unless it has been registered by the machine.

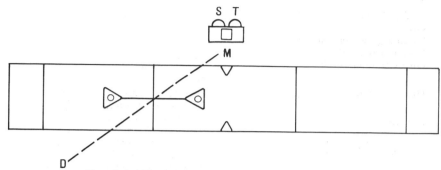

Fig. 6.4   Placement of Officials—Electric Foil. As fencers move, the director (D) must maintain a position that permits him or her to see the scoring machine as well as the fencers.

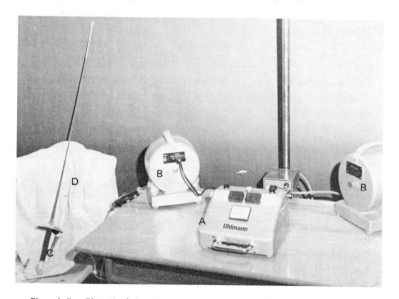

Fig. 6.5   Electrical Scoring Apparatus for Foil. A. Scoring machine; B. Reels are placed at each end of the strip and connected to the machine; C. Body cord which is worn inside the sleeve of each fencer, attaching to the reel in back, and to the foil; D. Metallic vest which is grounded to differentiate between valid hits to the vest and nonvalid hits to other parts of the body.

If only a white light turns on, an off-target touch has been made against the fencer on whose side the light appears. If only a colored light registers, a valid touch was made against the fencer on whose side the light appears.

If both a colored light and white light register on the same side, an off-target touch was made before a valid one and no point may be awarded.

Do you know how to read the lights when scoring is by electrical equipment? What does it mean if both a colored light and a white light register on the same side? May the director overrule a signal light?

If lights appear on both sides, the director must determine the validity and award the touch accordingly or declare a simultaneous touch with no score.

Only the apparatus may determine materiality of a touch. If, however, the director suspects that a touch was indicated when none occurred, he may disregard the point if the electric equipment is found to be faulty. No touch may be awarded unless it registers, even if a fault in the equipment is found.

General Rules for Determining the Validity of Touches   The director alone decides on validity of touches in the event that both fencers are touched. The fencers may not question the director's judgment about what occurred, but they may question the application of rules in view of what the director and the judges say took place. The following are the basic right-of-way rules that must be used in determining validity.

Article 233

Observance of the fencing phrase.

233 (a) Every correctly executed attack must be parried or completely avoided, and the phrase d'armes must be followed through.

To judge the correctness of an attack, the following points must be considered:

1. if the attack starts when the opponent is "in line" (i.e., "with the arm extended and the point threatening a valid surface"), the attacker must first deflect his adversary's weapon;

2. if the attack starts when the opponent is not in line, it may be executed either by a direct thrust or by a disengagement, or by a cutover (coupé), or may be preceded by effective feints that force the opponent to parry;

3. if, in searching for the opposing blade to deflect it, the blade is not found (derobement or trompement), the right-of-way passes to the opponent.

234 (b) The parry gives the right-of-way to the riposte; the simple riposte may be direct or indirect, but to annul any subsequent action of the attacker, it must be executed immediately, without indecision or delay.

235 (c) In a composite attack, if the opponent finds the blade on one of the feints, he has the right to riposte.

236 (d) In composite attacks, the opponent has the right to make a stop; but to be valid the stop must precede the conclusion of the attack by a period of fencing time, i.e., the stop must touch before the attacker has commenced the last movement of the conclusion of the attack.

Judging

237 In applying these fundamental conventions of the foil, the director must judge as follows:

Whenever, in a phrase d'arms, the fencers are both touched simultaneously, there has been either a *simultaneous action* or a *double touch.*

The former is the result of simultaneous conception and execution of the attack by both fencers; in this case, the touches given are annulled for both fencers, even if one of them has touched an invalid surface.

The double touch, on the contrary, is the result of a faulty action on the part of one of the fencers.

Consequently, if there is not a period of fencing time between the two touches:

1. *The fencer attacked is alone counted as touched—*

(a) if he makes a stop into a simple attack;

(b) if, instead of parrying, he attempts to avoid being touched, and fails;

(c) if, after a successful parry, he pauses for a moment—which gives his opponent the right to resume his attack (redoublement, remise, or reprise);

(d) if, on a composite attack, he makes a stop without having the advantage of a period of fencing time;

(e) if, being in line (arm extended and point threatening a valid surface), after a beat or a taking of the blade which deflects his weapon, he attacks or replaces his blade in line instead of parrying a direct thrust made by the attacker.

2. *The attacker alone is counted as touched—*

(a) if he starts his attack when the opponent is in line (arm extended and point threatening a valid surface) without deflecting the opposing blade;

(b) if he attempts to find the blade and fails (because of a derobement or trompement) and still continues the attack;

(c) if, in a composite attack, in the course of which his opponent finds the blade, he continues the attack while his opponent immediately ripostes;

(d) if, in a composite attack, he hesitates for a moment during which the opponent delivers a stop thrust, yet he continues his attack;

(e) if, in a composite attack, he is hit by a stop made with the advantage of a period of fencing time before his conclusion;

(f) if he touches by remise, redoublement, or reprise, after a parry by his opponent which is followed by an immediate simple riposte executed in one period of fencing time and withdrawal of the arm.[1]

---

1. *Fencing Rules: Authorized English Translation of the International* (FIE) *Rules.* Adopted by the Amateur Fencers League of America and the National Collegiate Athletic Association, 33 Sixty-second St., West New York, New Jersey 07093, 1974. pp. 42-43. Used by permission of Stephen B. Sobel, president, AFLA.

In competition it is illegal to remove your mask before the director's decision is made. Do you know the reasons for this rule? What is the penalty for violation of the rule?

SCORING

Touches are recorded against the fencer who has been scored upon, so that the fencer who first receives a score of five loses.

Scoring for Individual Meets

Individual meets are usually round-robin tournaments in which each fencer competes against every other person within the meet or pool. If more than ten fencers are competing, there must be a preliminary round or rounds consisting of two or more smaller pools. In championship tournaments, 50 percent or more of the competitors from each pool must advance. In class or intramural tournaments, however, the number of fencers per pool and the number that advances may be modified to suit the given situation.

OFFICIAL SCORE SHEET

	BARRAGE	No.	1	2	3	4	V	D	HR.	PL.
WEAPON		1								
COMPETITION		2								
POOL		3								
DATE		4								
DIRECTOR										

CLUB	FENCER	No.	1	2	3	4	5	6	7	8	9	10	V	D	HR.	PL.
		1				⊞⊥ D										
		2				⊢										
		3														
		4	⊥⊥ V													
		5			⊢											
		6														
		7														
		8														
		9														
		10														
		HG.														

Fig. 6.6 Round Robin Score Sheet

There is a specified "order of bouts" to be followed in a fencing meet (see fig. 6.7). When the correct order of bouts is followed and the pools consist of five or more people, no fencer will have to fence two consecutive bouts. In accordance with the example shown in figure 6.6, when there are six fencers, their names are written in the second column. The first bout is between fencers one and four. The scorer announces it and then the next, on deck, bout, which is between fencers two and five. The scorer should draw a horizontal line through each frame of the bout in progress if a line does not already appear. To determine which frames to use, find the intersecting frame by reading across from fencer number one

4 FENCERS 6 BOUTS	5 FENCERS 10 BOUTS	6 FENCERS 15 BOUTS		7 FENCERS 21 BOUTS		8 FENCERS 28 BOUTS		
1—4	1—2	1—4	6—4	1—4	3—1	2—3	8—3	3—7
2—3	3—4	2—5	1—2	2—5	4—6	1—5	6—7	4—8
1—3	5—1	3—6	3—4	3—6	7—2	7—4	4—2	2—6
2—4	2—3	5—1	5—6	7—1	3—5	6—8	8—1	3—5
3—4	5—4	4—2	2—3	5—4	1—6	1—2	7—5	1—7
1—2	1—3	3—1	1—6	2—3	2—4	3—4	3—6	4—6
	2—5	6—2	4—5	6—7	7—3	5—6	2—8	8—5
	4—1	5—3		5—1	6—5	8—7	5—4	7—2
	3—5			4—3	1—2	4—1	6—1	1—3
	4—2			6—2	4—7	5—2		
				5—7				

9 FENCERS 36 BOUTS				10 FENCERS 45 BOUTS				
1—9	1—2	3—1	4—1	1—4	7—8	3—4	8—1	6—4
2—8	9—3	2—4	5—3	6—9	5—1	8—9	7—4	9—5
3—7	8—4	5—9	6—2	2—5	10—6	5—10	9—3	10—3
4—6	7—5	8—6	9—7	7—10	4—2	1—6	2—6	7—1
1—5	6—1	7—1	1—8	3—1	9—7	2—7	5—8	4—8
2—9	3—2	4—3	4—5	8—6	5—3	3—8	4—10	2—9
8—3	9—4	5—2	3—6	4—5	10—8	4—9	1—9	3—6
7—4	5—8	6—9	2—7	9—10	1—2	6—5	3—7	5—7
6—5	7—6	8—7	9—8	2—3	6—7	10—2	8—2	1—10

Fig. 6.7 Order of Bouts to Be Followed in a Round Robin Meet

to the fourth frame. All touches against number one will be marked there. Likewise, read from fencer number four across to the coordinate of number one, and mark touches against number four in that frame. In short, read across to see who was touched and down to see by whom. In the example, figure 6.6, number four won, five to two. A **V** for victory or **D** for defeat is entered, and the next bout is called.

When all the bouts have been fenced, total victories and defeats are recorded in the columns to the right of the scores. The fencer with the most victories wins. In the event of a tie for first place, there is a fence-off to determine the winner. The inset score frame at the upper right of the regular score frame may be used for this barrage (fig. 6.6). Indicators are used to determine all other places in the event of ties. The total of all touches given minus all touches received determines place. The greater the difference, the better the score.

Team Scoring

A team may consist of three, four, or five men or women. International teams have four fencers, while most AFLA teams consist of three. Collegiate teams sometimes have five members for dual meets, but it is probably more common to have three. In a team match, every fencer on one team fences every fencer on the other, so a match between two teams of three fencers each would consist of nine bouts. Sixteen bouts would be needed for a four-man team and twenty-five for a five-man team.

The NCAA rules contain a simplified method of recording scores for a team match.[2]

	SCHOOL				SCHOOL		
No.	**Name**	**Score**		**No.**	**Name**	**Score**	
1.	Josephs	III	V	1.	Alberts	⊥⊥⊥	D
2.	Michaels	⊥⊥⊥	D	2.	Fredericks	II	V
3.	Johns	IIII	V	3.	Thomas	⊥⊥⊥	D
1.	Josephs	⊥⊥⊥	D	2.	Fredericks	O	V
2.	Michaels	I	V	3.	Thomas	⊥⊥⊥	D
3.	Johns	⊥⊥⊥	D	1.	Alberts	II	V
1.	Josephs	O	V	3.	Thomas	⊥⊥⊥	D
2.	Michaels	⊥⊥⊥	D	1.	Alberts	IIII	V
3.	Johns	II	V	2.	Fredericks	⊥⊥⊥	D
	Total Victories	**5**			Total Victories	**4**	

2. *Fencing Rules: Authorized English Translation of the International* (FIE) *Rules,* adopted by the Amateur Fencers League of America and the National Collegiate Athletic Association. 33 Sixty-second St., West New York, N.J. 07093, 1974.

If two fencers have tied for first place, how is the winner determined? How are ties for other places broken?

Scores should be announced after each touch is recorded so that the fencers and director can clearly hear them. If an error is made by the scorer, it must be corrected immediately because the score is official after the bout. Fencers may ask for a correction at the time a touch is made and recorded, but they may not protest the scoring of any previous point, so they should be aware of the score, as should the director.

SUGGESTED REFERENCES

Amateur Fencers League of America. *American Fencing Magazine.* AFLA: West New York, New Jersey.

Fencing Rules: Authorized English Translation of the International Rules. Adopted by the Amateur Fencers League of America and the National Collegiate Athletic Association. West New York, New Jersey, 1974.

Unwritten laws of fencing

7

During the so-called Age of Chivalry in the sixteenth century, the popularity of dueling went hand in hand with the development of fencing into a fine art as fencers realized the necessity of improving their skill. The sword became a gentleman's badge that was worn only by nobility who practiced diligently to become adept in its use. Noblewomen also studied fencing, and there are recorded instances of duels between women. The courtesies of fencing practice and of dueling were elaborate and precise, which was in keeping with the elevated station of the participants.

Fencing etiquette today reflects the general spirit that prevailed in the heyday of fencing. Fencing is still a sport for people who conduct themselves as ladies and gentlemen, and the accepted standards of fencing conduct are universal.

Until the early twentieth century, fencing form and sportsmanship were considered as important as scoring. Tournaments were judged on the basis of form, much as gymnastics is judged today; the manner in which one made an attack or defense was as important as whether or not it succeeded.

Fencers were required to acknowledge touches against themselves and were penalized if judges saw a touch that the recipient did not admit.

Today the criterion on which a fencer is judged is the more realistic one of whether or not a point lands, but poor sportsmanship and unnecessary roughness can still cost a fencer points.

There are not many rules of conduct, but the comprehensive written and unwritten laws of etiquette are taught and adhered to in all reputable fencing centers throughout the world.

CONDUCT OF THE FENCERS

Fencers always salute each other before putting on their masks. In a tournament the director, the audience, and then the opponent are quickly saluted. At the end of a bout, fencers remove their masks and shake non-sword hands.

Fig. 7.1   After a bout, fencers shake non-sword hands.

Informal Bouting

During informal play in the classroom or *salle d'armes*, fencers are expected to acknowledge all touches against themselves, whether valid or off target. A fencer does not claim touches against the opponent, but he may refuse to accept a point if, in his opinion, it was not a good touch.

Tournament Fencing

In a tournament a fencer may acknowledge a touch against himself, but usually fencers remain silent when they are touched. A fencer never challenges the opinion of the judge or the director about what occurred.

It is considered unsportsmanlike to attempt to influence a judge in any way, directly or indirectly. A fencer should not, for instance, rub his arm or leg to convince a judge that a touch was off target or pretend to straighten his blade after an attack to indicate that a point should be called. Nor should a fencer stop fencing and obviously wait for his judge to indicate that his attack was successful. If a fencer does stop to wait for a call, he may be touched.

If a fencer turns and walks away after an attack, it is proper for his opponent to touch him on the back. A fencer stops at his own risk. If a fencer scores cleanly and correctly, the touch will be called. If a fencer sometimes disagrees with a decision, he must realize that the jury is often better able to judge what happened than he is, and that each competitor probably equally shares the burden of the few inevitable mistakes that occur. The best fencers rely on ability, not on dramatics, in order to win.

A fencer may ask politely for an explanation of a decision, but he may not challenge whether a touch landed or not, or who had right-of-way.

Tension often mounts as fencers wait for the proper moment to attack. Their concentration is intense, and to competitors each point is of the utmost importance, so occasional outbursts do occur; however, a fencer must not violate the basic rules of courtesy and good sportsmanship.

A fencer may not remove his mask before a decision is made by the director. This rule is in the interest of safety as well as of sportsmanship. After a warning, a penalty point may be awarded against a fencer who takes the mask off before decision is rendered.

CONDUCT OF THE SPECTATORS

The audience at a fencing tournament acts similarly to that at a tennis match. Spectators must not try to influence officials or instruct contestants in any way, although they may applaud a well-executed attack. For the most part, quiet is necessary so that the fencers can hear the commands of the director and so that their attention will not be unduly diverted by excessive noise. The director can demand silence or may, in extreme situations, exclude members of the audience who do not conform to these standards.

HOW TO KNOWLEDGEABLY WATCH A FENCING BOUT

In order to follow the action during a bout, a spectator should pick one fencer and concentrate on his actions. Why did he attack when he did? What was his distance? How did he bait a trap to draw the other person's reaction? By identifying with one person, it is easier at first to watch the action develop. Later, a spectator may try to analyze action along with the director. Who made the attack? Was it parried or otherwise prevented from arriving? See if the director is usually in agreement with you. Fencing can be an exciting sport to watch critically, but your interest will lag soon if you don't understand the action or if you do not watch for some specific thing. Read up on the basic object of the sport and became familiar with its terminology if you plan to watch more than to participate.

Selection of equipment

8

Fencing equipment is relatively inexpensive and with care should last for many years. Although many schools furnish the clothing and equipment needed, anyone who seriously wants to fence should invest in his or her own personal equipment. All necessary clothing and equipment can be purchased from most fencing *salles* or clubs. Any school or fencing group can advise you regarding your fencing needs.

JACKET

The jacket is a vital part of your uniform and should be of good quality. Any manufacturer of fencing clothing must adhere to the minimum safety standards that are required by the rules. Half jackets or plastrons can be purchased at less cost than a full jacket, but since these could never be used in a tournament and do not afford full protection, they are not a good buy for an individual who cares enough about fencing to invest in his own clothing.

Jackets may be made of heavy gabardine, duck, canvas, or the new stretch fabrics. Most women prefer the gabardine because it looks nice and tends to be more comfortable to wear. Some women's jackets have the necessary padding sewn in as part of the garment, and some have an extra vest of heavy, quilted material which is worn under the outer jacket. In any case, women are required to have breast protectors of rigid material in addition to their jacket padding. Men may choose any of the fabrics, but if they plan to use épée, the duck, canvas, or stretch fabric will be necessary since the gabardine will tear more easily when struck by the stiffer blade of the épée.

The jacket should fit as snugly as possible without restricting movement. If a jacket is too large, there will be loose cloth that will make it easier for a point to catch on the fabric. Left-handed fencers should buy jackets that button on the right side and are padded on the left.

UNDERARM PROTECTOR

Because the electric foil is stiffer and heavier than the standard foil, regulations now require that men and women wear an underarm protector in addition to the padded jacket to provide extra protection.

TROUSERS

According to the rules, fencing trousers must be white and must fasten below the knees. While it is best to wear regulation trousers that are lightly padded on top of the leading thigh, you may begin fencing with any white trousers that will allow freedom of movement and will protect the legs. Later you can purchase fencing knickers, which match the jacket, allow for a maximum of motion, resist tearing, and look neat.

GLOVE

The foil glove should be of soft leather with a cuff that completely covers the lower part of the jacket sleeve. The glove may be lightly padded on the back. There also may be two thicknesses of leather on the end of the thumb and at the base of the thumb where the most wear occurs.

FOIL

When selecting a foil, you should pick one that is neither too heavy and inflexible nor too light and whippy. The foible of the blade should bend readily or the blade may break easily; however, if the blade is overly flexible, the point will be difficult to control.

If you will be fencing with electric foils at all, you should practice either with an electric foil or with a dummy electric blade; the latter is weighted the same as the electric foil but is less expensive. The dummy blade can be put into any standard mounting. It is a mistake to buy a light standard foil for practice if you will fence with the electric blade in competition because you will lose your accuracy when you switch from a light to a heavy weapon, and you will tire more easily if you are not used to

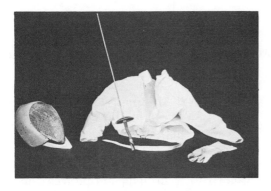

Fig. 8.1   Foil, mask, jacket, and glove are sufficient gear for a beginning fencer. (Photo by Robert Stadd)

the extra weight. If possible, every fencer should have two foils so that if one breaks, he has a spare.

MASK

A good-quality mask is an absolute necessity for safety's sake. A new, medium weight mask will be adequate since the manufacturers must conform to strict standards. The mask should be white or of a light color as specified in the rule book. The prices of masks vary somewhat, but this is partly because of the various trims used on them. Masks made of canvas with plastic trim are the least expensive and will serve quite well. Leather trim is more costly, more durable, and looks a little better, but it is not necessary. Plastic interior trim is the easiest to keep clean, but it is not quite as comfortable to wear as cloth. In any case, the bib should contain several thicknesses of material to protect the neck. The mask should feel comfortable to the wearer and be secure.

If a man wishes to fence épée or sabre as well as foil, there are three-weapon masks that have a heavier mesh and afford more protection for the top and back of the head.

Whenever any rust appears on a mask, it should be discarded for safety reasons. A mask that has been weakened by rust may be pierced by a heavy hit, and this could result in a severe injury to the fencer. For this reason it is unwise to buy a used mask. A mask is a personal item that you will want to keep for your own use.

ELECTRIC EQUIPMENT

If you decide to purchase the items necessary for electric foil fencing, you will need at least one, and preferably two, electric foils and at least two body cords. When you enter any electric tournament, you will be required to have two weapons and body cords in working condition.

The wires used in the electric foil and cord are relatively fine and do break occasionally. An armorer is an expert on maintenance and repair of electric equipment and will advise you. An armorer is required at every electrically scored meet.

A metallic vest is required for electric foil fencing. There must not be any tears in this vest, and it must fit so that it exactly corresponds to the valid target. It should be lined to insulate a perspiring fencer against receiving a mild shock when a point is made against him or her.

CARE OF EQUIPMENT

Fencing clothing will last longer and look better if it is kept clean. Jackets and gloves should be stored so that they will dry after they have been used.

Masks also should be kept clean and dry. Many masks have removable bibs to make laundering easier. If the bib does not snap out, it can be scrubbed without harming the mask if it is well dried after scrubbing. Never immerse the entire mask in water.

Foils should be stored in a dry place to prevent the formation of rust. They may be hung, point down, or stored so that they rest on the pommel, but they should never rest on the point.

Fencing bags are available for carrying equipment, but if your wet clothing, mask, and foil are all left rolled together after you have used them, the clothing will mildew and the metal objects will soon rust. Transport equipment in the bags, but remove it for permanent storage unless it is dry. With reasonable care, your fencing equipment should last for many years.

Where to find fencing

9

In Europe fencing traditionally has been a major sport and still is today. The Western Europeans have been consistent winners in international tournaments, although in recent years Poland, Hungary, and Russia have dominated Olympic and World Championship events. In those countries children begin fencing at an early age, and the best of them continue to fence competitively.

In America, fencing is a rapidly growing sport with more and more active participants each year. There are fencing clubs and *salles* in every major city in the United States where men, women, and children can learn to fence and continue to practice. Fencing is receiving additional impetus through efforts of the American Alliance for Health, Physical Education, and Recreation, which is sponsoring a Lifetime Sports Education Project, aimed at increasing national participation in sports such as fencing that may be enjoyed throughout life.

An ever-increasing number of colleges and high schools is offering fencing as more and more people are becoming involved in this fascinating sport.

There are many sources of information on fencing. You may find active fencing groups in your community through colleges and universities, the YMCA, YWCA, recreation centers, athletic clubs, or even telephone directories, which may list fencing schools.

AMATEUR FENCERS LEAGUE OF AMERICA

The Amateur Fencers League of America (AFLA) governs all fencing in this country. Divisions have been established throughout the nation to administer local fencing groups and tournaments.

Can you recall the title of the organization that governs fencing in the United States? If you have been ranked as a Class C fencer, may you compete in a Class B tournament? a Class A tournament? an unclassified tournament?

Regularly scheduled foil tournaments for women and tournaments in all three weapons for men are held within these divisions from September to June. Divisional winners in all open events qualify for the national championships, which are held annually in the latter part of June. National rankings and international team membership are determined from the results of the divisional and national championship tournaments.

Classification of Fencers

Fencers are classified by the AFLA according to their tournament performance. Class A is the highest ranking, followed by classes B and C, and the lowest ranking is Unclassified. A fencer may fence in any tournament that is specified as that person's classification or a higher one, but one may not fence in a lower classification. This system offers ample opportunity for less experienced fencers to compete against outstanding opponents, but it also allows them a chance to win on their own level.

COLLEGE FENCING IN AMERICA

Collegiate fencing has been increasing in quality as well as in quantity. Many schools on the East and West coasts have active competitive schedules, and there is a great deal of fencing throughout the Midwest as well. It is becoming increasingly popular in the South and Southwest. For many schools competition begins in the fall and continues through to spring.

Women's championships are held on the East and West coasts in the spring. The largest and oldest such event is the Intercollegiate Women's Fencing Association Championship, which is held in April on the East Coast. The Women's Western Intercollegiate Fencing Conference, which is held in March or April, is the second largest collegiate championship tournament for women, and other similar conferences meet throughout the country.

The men's competitive season is climaxed by regional championships throughout the country and the annual National Collegiate Athletic Association (NCAA) national fencing championships. Held on the third weekend in March, they take place at a different university each year.

INTERNATIONAL FENCING

All international fencing falls under the jurisdiction of the Federation International d'Escrime (FIE), with which the AFLA is affiliated. United States fencers have gained much international prestige over years. Although this country has not won any Olympic fencing events, it has had finalists and medalists in every weapon. Miguel A. de Capriles served as president of the FIE from 1961-1965, the first and only American to be so honored.

SUGGESTED REFERENCE

AMATEUR FENCERS LEAGUE OF AMERICA. *American Fencing Magazine.* AFLA: West New York, New Jersey.

The language and lore of fencing

10

Most fencing terms describe the actions to which they refer. Many of the terms in common usage in this country reflect the French or Italian origins of fencing, and although much of its terminology has been adapted or translated to English, many words are European. All international fencing championships are conducted in French, which is the international language of fencing, so the French influence predominates in terminology. Any real student of fencing should become familiar with the fencing vocabulary.

Most forms of attack and defense were first introduced many years ago by European fencing masters, many of whom sold their secret attacks or defenses to duelists who were willing to pay dearly for them. Usually the student was instructed behind closed doors and was sworn to secrecy so that these tricks would not become general knowledge, for then they would be less effective. Today's fencing is largely made up of refinements and modifications of these old actions which, through the years, have proved themselves to be the best means of attack and defense.

Abstain. A judge may "abstain" or decline to vote if he was unable to see whether or not a point was made.

Absence of the blade. When the blades are not engaged.

Advance. To move forward in the guard position.

Amateur Fencers League of America (AFLA). This is the governing body of amateur fencing in the United States. It establishes rules and regulations and selects teams for international competitions. Founded in 1891, the AFLA is affiliated with the Federation Internationale d'Escrime.

Attack. An initial attempt to hit the opponent.

Attack on the blade. An action, such as a beat, press, or bind, that removes the opponent's blade from line to clear the way for an attack.

Attack on preparation. An attack that is made as the opponent makes a beat, change, feint, or advance in preparation for his attack. This attack must begin before the opponent's attack actually begins.

Ballestra. A jump-lunge attack. This term suggests the historic link between fencing and the formal ballet, which is said to have been influenced by the basic fencing positions.

Barrage. A fence-off of a tie between two or more fencers.

Beat. A sharp tap against the opponent's blade to clear the way for an offensive action.

Bind (Liément). An action that removes a threatening blade by binding it, or carrying it from high line to the opposite low line by crossing the blade over the opponent's blade to hit in the low line with opposition. If the bind is executed vigorously enough, it may be used to disarm an opponent. Disarming an opponent, however, is no longer advantageous since action stops whenever a weapon is dropped. In the days of dueling and of early fencing, this was a valuable trick to master. Today it is a useful action, but no attempt is made to actually disarm a fencer by this means.

Call. A signal to stop the bout. If a fencer wishes to stop during a bout without danger of being hit, he or she may "call" to the director to stop the bout by quickly stamping his or her forward foot two times.

Change of engagement. The act of going from one line to engage the blade in another.

Closed line. A line that is protected by the blade and arm.

Compound attack. Any attack consisting of two or more actions. It also may be called a composed attack.

Corps-à-corps (clinch). Literally body-to-body, in which there is body contact or a closing of the guards so that normal fencing actions become impossible.

Coulé (glide). A preparatory action that is made by gliding along the side of the opponent's blade.

Counter attack. A stop thrust in which the time is taken from the attacker by touching before the final action of the original attack begins.

Counter parry. A circular parry that is made by parrying in the side opposite the one to which an attack is made.

Counter riposte. An offensive action that follows the successful parry of a riposte.

Counter time. A second-intention attack.

Coupé (cutover). A simple attack that is made by lifting the blade over the opponent's blade to hit in the opposite line.

Croise. An action similar to the bind in which the blade crosses over a menacing blade to carry it from a high line to the low line on the same side. This action is used in preference to a bind as a stop thrust with opposition because it is quicker since it does not draw the other blade across the target.

Derobement (deception). An evasion of the opponent's attempt to engage or beat the blade.

Direct. Indicates than an attack or parry is made without changing lines.

Disengage. A simple attack that is made by leaving the line of engagement to hit in another.

Double. A compound attack in which the attacker feints a disengage and deceives a counter parry. This may be described as a corkscrew attack.

Engagement. The contact of two opposing blades.

Envelopment. A double bind that envelops the opposing, menacing blade in motion that carries it in a complete circle to land in the line of the original engagement.

False attack. A lunge that is made to draw a response without the intention of landing.

Feint. A pretended attack that is made by a menacing extension of the foil arm. It is made preparatory to an attack in order to draw a response.

Fencing time. The time required to make one simple fencing action. This time will vary according to the speed of the fencers in question.

Federation Internationale d'Escrime (FIE). The governing body of all international fencing tournaments. This organization was founded in Europe in the latter part of the nineteenth century at which time some rules were set up to govern tournaments.

Flèche. A running attack. The literal translation from French is "arrow," which aptly describes this as a swift, flying attack.

Foible. The flexible, or point half, of the blade.

Forte. The strong half of the blade that extends from the guard.

Lines. The four theoretical areas of the target: upper inside and outside and lower inside and outside.

Lunge. An extension of the guard position made in order to reach the opponent. The lunge was introduced during the last part of the sixteenth century as a new secret form of attack.

Mask. The protective wire helmet that is worn on the head. The first masks were made from sheet metal with eye slits cut out of them. These were never widely used because they were uncomfortable and very dangerous —the eye was vulnerable to hits because the metal allowed the point to slide to the eye slits. Some right-of-way conventions of fencing stem from the premask days when, for instance, it was considered wrong to riposte until the opponent had recovered from the lunge because to do so would have been extremely hazardous. The first wire masks were used around 1800.

Match. A contest between two teams.

Off-target hit. A point hit which does not land on the valid target. This term is now preferred to the term *foul.*

On guard. The basic ready fencing position.

One-two. A compound attack that consists of feinting a disengage and then disengaging to deceive a direct parry.

Parry. A defensive action that deflects the attacker's blade.

Passé. When the foil point grazes the target rather than hits it squarely.

Pattinando. A quick advance-lunge.

Piste (strip). From the French word meaning "path." This is the fencing area. It may be said to resemble a path or strip because of its long, narrow shape.

Phrase or phrase d'armes. A period of continuous fencing that may consist of many actions by one or both fencers. When there is any break in play, a phrase ends.

Pommel. The metal part at the end of the handle that fastens the parts of the foil together and also acts as a counterweight to the blade, thereby making it a balanced weapon.

President (director). The individual who presides over a fencing meet.

Pressure. A preliminary motion made by applying a slight pressure against the opponent's blade to cause a reaction that will open the way for an attack.

Prise-de-fer. A taking of the opponent's blade. This refers to blade contact.

Redoublement. A new offensive action made against a fencer who defends without riposting.

Remise. An immediate continuation of an attack that was parried or fell short. It is made without withdrawing the arm, usually while in a lunge.

Reprise. A new attack made after returning to the guard position.

Right-of-way. The right to attack. It goes to the fencer who first extends his arm or initiates an attack or who parries an attack.

Riposte. An answering attack made by a fencer after he has successfully defended himself.

Second-intention attack. A false attack intended to draw a parry-riposte that the original attacker then parries so he can hit on a counter riposte. The attacker intends throughout the action to hit on his second attack.

Semicircular parry. A parry from high to low line or vice versa, so called because the point travels in an arc to make the parry.

Simple attack. An attack consisting of just one motion. There are three simple attacks: straight thrust, disengage, and cutover.

Stop thrust. A counter attack made by extending into a poorly executed attack. In order to be valid, a stop must arrive before the final motion of the attack begins.

Straight thrust. A direct, simple attack that consists of a lunge to hit without changing the line of engagement.

Strip (piste). The field of play. The strip is usually made of rubber so that fencers will not slip as they move. In electric fencing meets, the strip may be covered with wire mesh that grounds any hits to the floor that would otherwise register as off target.

Thrust. The action of hitting with an extended arm. To make a firm thrust the point is placed on the target with the action of the fingers.

Touch. A valid point hit against the opponent.

Valid touch. A point hit that lands on the target area without having first landed off target.

SUGGESTED REFERENCES

Fencing Rules: Authorized English Translation of the International Rules. Adopted by the Amateur Fencers League of America and the National Collegiate Athletic Association. West New York, New Jersey, 1974.

GARRET, MAXWELL R., and HEINECKE, MARY. *Fencing.* Boston: Allyn and Bacon, 1971.

PALFFY-ALPAR, JULIUS. *Sword and Masque.* Philadelphia: F. A. Davis Co., 1967.

Appendix: Questions and answers

MULTIPLE CHOICE

1. Fencing began to develop as a sport after
   a. dueling was outlawed
   b. archer's accuracy with the bow and arrow made swordfighting obsolete
   C. gunpowder came into common use
   d. a duel in which a powerful French nobleman was killed by a sword (p. 1)
2. The rules of which modern weapon most closely resemble real dueling?
   a. foil   B. épée   c. sabre   d. rapier (p. 3)
3. With which weapon(s) do women most often compete?
   A. foil   b. épée   c. sabre   d. foil and épée (p. 2)
4. With which weapon(s) may "cuts" be made?
   a. foil   b. épée   C. sabre   d. épée and sabre (p. 3)
5. Which is the heaviest weapon?
   a. foil   c. sabre
   B. épée   d. there is no weight difference (p. 3)
6. Which of the following is not a part of the foil?
   A. points d'arret   d. foible
   b. pommel   e. bell
   c. forte   (p. 8)
7. The governing body of fencing in this country is the
   a. AFCC   B. AFLA   c. CIO   d. AAF   e. FIE (p. 80)
8. Breakage of foil blades may be kept at a minimum by
   a. using very stiff blades
   b. hitting squarely so that the blade will not bend
   c. replacing blades every month
   D. allowing the hand to "give upwards" so the blade will bend up (p. 26)
9. In the guard position, the proper distance between the feet is
   A. about shoulder width   c. about one foot
   b. about two feet   d. the most natural stance (p. 11)
10. The advance is
    a. made by moving first the back foot and then the front foot forward one
       step

b.   made by moving both feet simultaneously forward
C.   made by moving the front foot first and then back
d.   begun by rocking the weight forward (p. 12)

11. In an effective lunge, the rear leg is extended
a.   to lower the center of gravity
B.   to provide the force for the lunge
c.   for aesthetic reasons
d.   to complete the lunge (p. 15)

12. The lunge
a.   should be as long as physically possible
B.   is an extension of the guard position to reach the opponent
c.   is never used in a riposte
d.   is necessary to score a point (p. 13)

13. "Fingering," which refers to the control of the point of the foil, is achieved by
A.   use of thumb and forefinger
b.   a tight wrist action
c.   rotating the hand from the wrist
d.   pressing alternately with three guide fingers and thumb (p. 22)

14. The foil should be held
a.   loosely at all times
b.   by the thumb and forefinger
c.   tightly so it cannot be parried out of line
D.   in a firm, yet relaxed grip (p. 8)

15. In the relaxed guard position, the elbow of the sword arm should
a.   be tucked against the rib cage
b.   project beyond the outline of the body as viewed by the opponent
C.   be a hand's breadth from the body
d.   be "broken" just enough to keep the sword arm from rigidity (p. 12)

16. A good guard position permits the fencer to
a.   retreat more easily than advance
b.   advance more easily than retreat
C.   retreat or advance with equal ease
d.   attack more easily than defend (p. 12)

17. While in the guard position
a.   the hand is always kept to the left of the body for protection
b.   the point is as high as the top of the opponent's mask
C.   the hand moves left or right as necessary to protect any of the four lines
d.   the hand remains stationary (p. 19)

18. When in a full lunge, the forward knee should be
a.   in front of the toe   C.   over the instep
b.   over the toe   d.   behind the heel (p. 15)

19. When two fencers fence with foibles of their blades in contact, the blades are
A.   engaged   c.   on guard
b.   disengaged   d.   in fourth position (p. 18)

20. Correct fencing distance is
a.   with the points touching
b.   close enough to eliminate the necessity of lunging
c.   determined by the lunging distance of the shorter fencer
D.   determined by the lunging distance of the taller fencer (p. 16)

21. A "jump lunge" is called the
a.   passata de soto   d.   piroutte
b.   advance-lunge   e.   flèche
C.   ballestra (p. 32)

22. The act of going from six to engage the blade in four is called
    a. disengage
    b. double change
    C. change of engagement
    d. cutover   (p. 23)

23. In a simple attack, it is important to aim
    A. before extending the arm
    b. during the arm extension
    c. during the lunge
    d. at the instant the hit is made   (p. 26)

24. The three simple attacks are
    a. change of engagement, disengage, and coupé
    b. beat-coupé, beat-straight thrust, disengage
    C. straight thrust, disengage, and coupé
    d. disengage, coupé, and one-two   (pp. 26-27)

25. In a disengage, the lunge should begin
    a. before the point starts to change line
    b. as the point starts to change line
    C. as soon as the point is aimed
    d. after the beat   (p. 26)

26. Which of the following is a simple attack?
    a. beat-straight thrust
    B. coupé
    c. one-two
    d. double   (p. 27)

27. The feint is
    a. a parry
    b. an attack
    C. a pretended attack
    d. an attack without a lunge   (pp. 28-29)

28. In a feint, the arm is
    a. not extended
    B. extended
    c. not fully extended
    d. fully extended before the lunge (p. 28-29)

29. A compound attack is
    a. preceded by an advance
    b. always preceded by a beat
    c. the same as a riposte
    D. any attack of two or more actions (p. 28)

30. A beat may properly be used
    a. to clear the opponent's blade away before an attack
    b. to get the opponent to react, creating an opening for an attack
    c. to upset the opponent who is obviously getting set to attack
    D. any of these   (p. 29)

31. The one-two is
    a. preceded by a beat
    B. a feint of disengage and another disengage
    c. a feint of disengage to avoid a counter parry
    d. the avoiding of two counter parries   (p. 29)

32. The double is
    a. a simple attack
    b. a feint of disengage
    c. the avoiding of two direct parries
    D. a feint of disengage and a circle avoiding a counter parry   (p. 30)

33. An "attack to the blade" which is only made against an extended arm is the
    a. press   b. glide   c. disengage   D. bind   (p. 33)

34. The "press" is
    A. a preparatory action
    b. the same as a beat
    c. an attack
    d. a defense   (p. 29)

35. The "glide" may effectively be used against a fencer who
    a. has a heavy hand
    B. has a light hand
    c. fences with absence of the blade
    d. changes engagement often   (p. 29)

36. Advance attacks should not be used against
    a. a fencer who has a longer reach than you
    b. a fencer who can be relied on to retreat as you attack

C. a fencer who stands his or her ground when parrying
d. any of these   (p. 30)

37. The flèche is
A. a running attack   c. an illegal attack
b. a lunging attack   d. an example of poor fencing form
                                                                          (pp. 32-33)

38. The flèche should
a. not be used in foil
b. not be used in any weapon
C. be used sparingly
d. be used in preference to the lunge whenever the opponent can be counted
    on to retreat as he or she parries   (p. 32)

39. Taking a step in retreat each time an opponent attacks is
a. an easy method of evading a simple attack
b. a habit easily countered by a determined opponent
c. a dangerous tactic when near the end line
D. all of these   (p. 13)

40. The parry is
A. a defensive action   c. an offensive action
b. either offensive or defensive   d. any beat   (p. 23)

41. The inside lines are
a. four and six   c. six and eight
B. four and seven   d. six and seven   (pp. 19-22)

42. Semicircular parries are made when
a. moving from a guard of six to parry in four
b. taking a high-line counter parry
c. taking a low-line counter parry
D. moving from high line to parry in low line or vice versa   (p. 24)

43. If an attacker's arm withdraws during the attack
a. it does not count, even though it lands
b. it still has the right-of-way
C. the opponents may extend his or her arm and take the right-of-way
d. it is called an invalid touch   (p. 28)

44. The stop hit
a. is illegal
b. should be made against a simple attack
C. is usually dangerous
d. should be used only against a cutover   (p. 35)

45. If an opponent habitually retreats a step at each of your attacks, you may
    effectively
a. wait for that person to advance, attacking as he or she moves forward
b. gain ground and lunge again in your attack
c. make a ballestra attack
D. any of these   (p. 50)

46. If an attack fails, the fencer should
A. continue play until a point lands
b. retreat
c. return to the guard position and engage blades before continuing
d. close in to stop action   (p. 45)

47. If an opponent makes a fast disengage, it would usually be best to
a. retreat   d. parry and riposte
b. advance   E. retreat, parry, and riposte
c. extend the arm and try to hit first   (p. 36)

48. If an opponent is very aggressive making many composed attacks, it would be best for the fencer to
    A. wait for the attack and make a parry-riposte to score
    b. parry but not riposte
    c. extend his or her arm and hope to land first
    d. attack in an attempt to confuse the opponent   (p. 36)

49. In a regulation women's bout, the winner must score
    A. five touches
    b. the most out of a total of four touches
    c. four touches
    d. all she can in eight minutes fencing time   (p. 55)

50. The valid foil target excludes
    A. the head and arms   c. the left side
    b. the back   d. all of these   (p. 54)

51. The riposte
    a. has the right-of-way over an attack
    B. is an attack made by the defender after parrying the attack
    c. is a continuation of an attack after failure to land
    d. is not valid unless made with a lunge   (pp. 36, 65)

52. If an off-target hit is made
    a. it is a touch against the attacker
    b. it is a touch against the defender
    C. it stops all action immediately
    d. fencers stop and go to the center of the strip   (p. 54)

53. When a valid touch is made,
    a. fencers cross blades and resume action where they stopped
    B. fencers must stop and resume action in the center of the strip
    c. if there is a director, the one who scored the touch stops and waits for
       the director to acknowledge the point
    d. if there is a director, the fencer who is hit must stop and say "I am hit." (p. 56)

54. The foil strip is
    A. 6'7" by 46'   c. 4' by 20'
    b. 6'7" by 60'   d. 4' by 10'   (p. 53)

55. When a fencer backs off of the end of the strip with both feet after a warning
    A. he or she is declared touched
    b. fencers are stopped and brought in three feet
    c. he or she is declared touched unless it occurs on the last touch
    d. he or she is disqualified   (p. 56)

56. In an official, standard foil bout,
    a. the director may overrule all four judges
    B. the director may overrule one judge because he or she has 1 1/2 votes to
       1 vote each for the judges
    c. the judges must watch the right-of-way as well as touches
    d. the director has no vote but watches only validity   (p. 57)

57. In an official, standard foil bout,
    a. the judges must call out whenever they see a point land
    B. only the director may officially stop the bout, except in an emergency or
       when time runs out
    c. fencers are obliged to call touches received
    d. fencers should stop fencing if a point lands, called or not   (p. 59)

58. A bout is not stopped
    a. for an invalid touch   c. when a fencer goes off the strip
    B. when a hit lands   d. when a corps-à-corps exists   (p. 54)

59. This score sheet indicates that
    a. No 2 defeated No. 1
    b. No. 2 defeated No. 4
    c. No. 4 defeated No. 1
    D. No. 4 defeated No. 2
    e. No. 3 defeated No. 2

	1	2	3	4
1	▨		⌐III	
2		▨		III
3	II		▨	
4		III		▨

(p. 67)

60. Time has run out in a bout between two fencers, No. 1 and No. 3. The score will be
    a. 2-3, number 3 wins
    b. advanced to 5-2, number 1 wins
    c. advanced to 5-4, number 1 wins
    D. 5-4, number 3 wins
    e. as it stands with a double loss

(p. 55)

TRUE OR FALSE

t	F	61.	The best drill for improving fencing techniques is bouting practice. (pp. 41-42)
t	F	62.	Electrical scoring was developed primarily for spectator appeal. (p. 3)
t	F	63.	The ballestra is a salute which derives from ballet. (p. 32)
T	f	64.	The lunge should be preceded by an extended arm. (p. 13)
t	F	65.	It is not possible to "overlunge." (p. 15)
T	f	66.	Correct fencing distance is determined by lunging distance. (p. 16)
t	F	67.	The act of passing the point underneath the opponent's blade to engage it on the other side is called the disengage. (p. 23)
T	f	68.	The engagement in the upper outside line is that of sixth. (p. 19)
t	F	69.	There are eight common direct parries in foil fencing. (p. 19)
T	f	70.	A parry may be made by beat or by opposition. (p. 23)
T	f	71.	The bind should be used only on an opponent who has an extended arm. (p. 33)
T	f	72.	The flèche is most effective when it takes the opponent completely by surprise. (p. 33)
t	F	73.	A false attack is an illegal action. (p. 34)
T	f	74.	When you parry an attack, you gain right-of-way which entitles you to an immediate riposte. (p. 36)
t	F	75.	If an attack hits off target and an immediate riposte hits the valid target, the attacker shall receive a point against him or her. (p. 65)
t	F	76.	If an attacker hits off target, then immediately hits the valid target, the point shall be awarded. (p. 65)
t	F	77.	A fencer may gain right-of-way by extending his or her arm, point in line, or by advancing. (p. 65)
t	F	78.	If your opponent reacts to a feint-of-disengage with a counter parry, you can score by making either a one-two or a double. (p. 30)
T	f	79.	A second-intent attack is an effective tactic against an opponent who makes stop thrusts. (p. 50)
t	F	80.	An attack on preparation is a form of stop thrust. (p. 48)
T	f	81.	An attack on preparation may take advantage of your opponents lateral foil movements. (p. 48)
T	f	82.	The valid foil target is the same for men and women. (p. 54)

t F   83. The back is not a valid target.   (p. 54)

t F   84. A fencer may not switch hands during a bout under any circumstances.
                                                                               (p. 54)

T f   85. A corps-à-corps exists whenever there is bodily contact of any sort. (p. 81)

T f   86. Fencing at close quarters is allowed as long as weapons can be used
            correctly.   (p. 55)

t F   87. An off-target touch is the same as a flat touch.   (p. 54)

t F   88. A bout is stopped when the point grazes the target.   (p. 54)

t F   89. If a point lands fairly but bounces off the target, no touch is awarded.
                                                                               (p. 54)

T f   90. If the back hand is hit while it covers any part of the valid target, a good
            touch is called   (p. 55)

T f   91. If after one warning, a fencer again covers the valid target with the
            unarmed hand, a penalty touch should be scored against that fencer,
            even if the hand is not hit.   (p. 55)

t F   92. If two people attack at the same time with straight arms and both land
            at the same time, both are awarded a touch.   (p. 55)

T f   93. If an attack is parried and the defender does not reposte, the attacker
            may try to score again from the lunge position.   (p. 65)

t F   94. The riposte may be made only from the guard position.   (p. 36)

T f   95. A stop-hit into a continuous one-two attack does not take right-of-
            way.   (pp. 64-65)

t F   96. A remise has the right-of-way over a riposte.   (p. 65)

T f   97. When a fencer steps off the side of the strip with both feet, and when
            no touch is made, he is penalized one meter.   (p. 56)

t F   98. Displacing the target by ducking or turning is not allowed.   (pp. 48, 55)

T f   99. The Director of a bout is responsible for determining validity when
            both fencers are hit.   (p. 60)

T f   100. The Director of an electrically scored bout has more responsibility than
            in a standard bout in which judges may assist in decisions.   (p. 62)

ANSWERS TO EVALUATION QUESTIONS

*No answer

Page	Answer and Page Reference
4	The foil and épée are thrusting weapons. The foil is a light, flexible weapon, and the épée is stiff, heavy, and triangular in cross-section. The sabre is a cutting or thrusting blade with a simulated cutting edge along the entire front edge and one-third of the back edge. (p. 5-6)
5	The foil tip should be covered, the jacket must be buttoned, a glove should protect the hand, and a mask must be worn during any practice. (p. 2-3)
8	*
11	The French foil consists of: part A, pommel; part B, handle; part C, guard; part D, blade. (p. 8)
19	By passing the point of the foil under the opponent's blade to engage the blade on the opposite side. The point moves first to the other side of the blade, then the hand moves to the new guard position. (p. 23)
26	*

34 A blade taken in four is moved to eight, and a blade taken in six is moved to seven. (p. 34)

35 The bind. Yes, the bind is made only against an extended arm with a menacing point. A can defend by bending the arm to parry in seven or eight. (p. 34)

37 *

39 The point should be no higher than the chin when in the guard position. Parries should be made near the center of the blade. (p. 38)

41 *

48 When fencers are unable to use their weapons effectively or when a corps-à-corps exists. (p. 55)

51 Fencer B must gain right-of-way. He must cause A to withdraw his arm, or B must deflect A's point with a beat, press, or bind. (Not directly answered in the text)

57 The touch is valid because the director's 1 1/2 votes overrule the one judge's vote of 1. (p. 57)

60 Fencer A is touched if B had an extended arm which A did not deflect, or if B made a parry-riposte while A touched with a remise.
Fencer B is touched if he made a stop thrust into an attack. (p. 65)

64 If both lights on one side light up, an off-target hit arrived first, then a valid touch. The director may not overrule a signal light unless equipment is found to be faulty. (p. 64)

66 Yes. This rule was made primarily for safety reasons. The penalty for removing a mask without permission is, first, a warning, then a point against the offender. (p. 54)

69 When a tie for first place exists it must be fenced-off in a barrage. In ties for other places, total touches received are subtracted from total touches scored. The greater difference is the better score. (p. 68)

78 Amateur Fencers League of America.
A C class fencer may fence in a class A or B tournament, but not in an unclassified tournament that is a lesser classification. (p. 78)

Index

GV
1147
B 68

c.1

15,532

CAMROSE LUTHERAN COLLEGE
LIBRARY.